THIS BOOK SHOULD BE RETURNED O
DATE SHOWN TO THE LIBRARY FROM

AUTHOR | **CLASS**

TITLE

ITALY IN THE
SECOND WORLD WAR

ITALY IN THE SECOND WORLD WAR

MEMORIES AND DOCUMENTS

By

PIETRO BADOGLIO

Translated by

MURIEL CURREY

GEOFFREY CUMBERLEGE
OXFORD UNIVERSITY PRESS
London   New York   Toronto
1948

Oxford University Press, Amen House, London E.C. 4

EDINBURGH GLASGOW NEW YORK TORONTO MELBOURNE
WELLINGTON BOMBAY CALCUTTA MADRAS CAPE TOWN

Geoffrey Cumberlege, Publisher to the University

PRINTED IN GREAT BRITAIN

TO ALL THE ITALIANS
WHO IN THE STRUGGLE
AGAINST THE NAZI–FASCIST TYRANNY
HAVE OFFERED
THEIR LIVES, THEIR LABOUR,
AND THEIR SUFFERINGS
I DEDICATE MY PAGES
IN THE HOPE
THAT FROM THE SACRIFICE
THE COUNTRY WILL ARISE AGAIN
UNITED—FREE—RESPECTED

Preface

I HAVE written this book because I believe that the Italian people have the right to know the course of events which led to their ruin. I do not wish to try to justify myself. Only the man who acts makes mistakes.

BADOGLIO

Cava dei Tirreni, July 1944.

Contents

x   *Contents*

PART I

CHAPTER I

1939

IN April 1939 Mussolini sent a memorandum in his own handwriting to Hitler. Copies of this memorandum were forwarded to the King and to me. Mussolini declared that in his opinion a war would inevitably break out within a very short time between the rich and the poor nations, between those with a high birth-rate and those with a shrinking population, between those with large supplies of raw materials and those which were markedly deficient in raw materials. The Peace of Versailles, instead of remedying the situation, had greatly aggravated it; there was not, in his view, the slightest hope that a just solution would be arrived at by any conference. The outcome was inevitable and menacing—the choice was between fighting and dying of suffocation.

The preparation for this struggle, added Mussolini, must be far-reaching and thorough. As a result of the Ethiopian campaign and the continuing need for the suppression of revolts in that country, as well as her outstanding contribution in the Spanish civil war, Italy would need some years to complete her military preparations. He declared that neither the country nor the armed forces would be ready before 1943 to face what he believed would be a long and bitter struggle.

To these very grave statements he added another, which was absolutely puerile. He said that he had decided on the year 1943 so that the International Exhibition in Rome, which he had planned for 1942, could be held. He was

B

counting on the large quantities of foreign currency, which
visitors would bring into the country, to help to pay for the
war. In an atmosphere as gloomy as that of 1939 the success of such an Exhibition was very improbable; so it was
ridiculous to think that the profits could make a substantial contribution to the finances of the country and so enable her to pay for a long war.

This memorandum made a very painful impression on
me. What was the motive which inspired such a document? Certainly it was not the pressure of public opinion.
After the conquest of Ethiopia the people did not feel
themselves to be threatened by 'suffocation', nor was it
necessary as a posthumous revenge for the wrongs suffered
at Versailles. For good or ill Mussolini had himself
settled the outstanding questions by means of successive
treaties with England and France.

My explanation cannot be proved by mathematical
formulae, but it is consonant with the facts, and I have no
hesitation in expressing my personal conviction because
I believe it approximates to the truth.

During their first meeting at Venice, Hitler did not
make a good impression on Mussolini; he talked without
stopping for an hour, repeating in different words all the
arguments from *Mein Kampf*, and only allowing Mussolini
a few minutes in which to reply. Mussolini himself told me,
when he got back to Rome, that Hitler was simply a
gramophone with seven records, and that when he had
played them all he began again at the beginning. He said
the same thing to everyone who had accompanied him to
the interview and the catchword was repeated with admiration all over Rome by his 'incense-bearers'.

Privately, Mussolini's overweening belief in his own
genius had led him to believe that in any future collaboration between the two dictators he would play the leading

part, because of his intellectual superiority. And this conviction was shown publicly during his visit to Germany in 1937, when his bearing was that of a god descended from Olympus to shed the light of his countenance upon the people. But little by little the chatterer, the gramophone with seven records, although continuing to talk, began to act. He occupied the demilitarized zone of the Rhineland, he armed numerous divisions, he created an enormous air force, and finally he seized Austria, the Sudetenland, and Czechoslovakia. Mussolini had to reassert his rightful position, to make Hitler understand that only the Italian Dictator had the ability and the prestige to direct affairs.

This was the motive which inspired his memorandum; it seemed to ignore any inconvenient facts, while facing the future with confidence and laying down the lines to be followed.

I am not claiming supernatural power of intuition— Mussolini had an overwhelming pride and believed himself to be immeasurably superior to the rest of mankind. I will give one example of this belief. In 1925 or 1926 he sent out an excellent circular on the powers and duties of the prefects. It remained a dead letter. When I asked him if he had drafted it, he replied with some annoyance: 'Who else would have had the brains?'

As far as I know, Hitler never answered the memorandum. When I received it I went to see Mussolini to explain my views. For five years the Army had had an excellent Minister for War, General Gazzera; he was inclined to be harsh but he was upright, conscientious, very far-sighted, and experienced. But despite all these qualities he was dismissed from office because he had never yielded to pressure from the Fascist Party, and the portfolio was taken over by Mussolini. This, however, was a mere formality, the real power was in the hands of the Under-

Secretary. Successive holders of this post were Baistrocchi[1]
and Pariani and their methods had disastrous results. The
first, entirely regardless of all regulations, introduced
politics into the Army and laid down that promotion was
to depend on loyalty to the Fascist Party. Pariani, a man
of lively but undisciplined intelligence, threw the whole
organization of the Army into confusion.

The training of the Air Force under the Under-Secretary, General Valle,[2] was more showy than practical, and
when General Pricolo succeeded he found after a careful
inquiry that of the 3,000 planes claimed by Valle only
1,200 existed, and of these at least 200 were out of date.

Only the Navy under Admiral Cavagnari was really
efficient.

I therefore told Mussolini that I could not agree that the
armed forces would be ready for war by 1943, the date
which he had given; I had, however, instructed the Chiefs
of Staffs of the three Services to study the various questions
and to draw up a programme of rearmament, conditional
on the capacity of our heavy industries. Mussolini assured
me that no financial considerations would stand in the way,
and that so far as the date was concerned it was merely a
general indication.

As soon as I got back to my office I drafted a letter to
him as I wished to make the essential points of such an important matter perfectly clear. I stated:

1. That, as he was aware, the armed forces, except for
   the Navy, were utterly unready.
2. That the essential question of new equipment must
   immediately be considered.
3. That only after the completion of the necessary plans,

[1] A prominent Fascist, a senior officer in the Militia, he had been promoted general during the Ethiopian campaign.

[2] Mussolini was Minister for Air. (*Translator.*)

and discussion with the armament firms, would it be possible to foresee with any accuracy the date by which the Army and the Air Force would be rearmed.

4. That for these reasons the year 1943 could not be regarded as definite for this purpose.

5. That I would arrange that he should be informed each week of the progress made.

6. That, as laid down by the Supreme Defence Committee, it was essential to proceed immediately with the purchase abroad of the raw materials which we required.

During July our ambassador in Berlin, Attolico, a very intelligent and far-sighted man, began to warn us that, as a result of information he had received from reliable sources, he was convinced that the Germans intended to attack Poland to settle, once and for all, the matters in dispute between the two countries. He added that Hitler and the leading Nazis were persuaded that the guarantee given by England and France to Poland represented merely a vague ideal and moral support, and that those two Powers would never declare war on Germany in support of Poland. This news aroused the liveliest emotions in the breast of Mussolini. Dictator Number Two had once again seized the conductor's baton.

At that time I had a long talk with Mussolini. He was furious over the political blindness of the Germans, saying, 'As a matter of fact only one German has shown any real political ability—Bismarck. It is obvious that von Ribbentrop does not understand anything. How could two such countries as England and France give a guarantee to Poland and then abandon her as soon as she is attacked!'

Ciano, the Minister for Foreign Affairs, was sent to

Germany to explain Mussolini's point of view by word of mouth. When he arrived for 'consultation' von Ribbentrop announced immediately in a tone which admitted of no discussion: 'We have decided to go to war.' Ciano gave a long account of this interview to the Chamber of Deputies,[1] so it is common knowledge.

But he said nothing in the Chamber about a letter from Hitler to Mussolini which he had brought back with him. The gist of the letter was:

War against Poland is inevitable, both to settle the question of the Corridor and to put an end to the ill-treatment of Germans by Poles. I am absolutely convinced that neither the English nor the French will risk their future for love of the Poles. But whether they enter the struggle or not, it is a purely Nordic matter, and Germany is able to handle it by herself. Italy in fact is not involved, and in addition her military preparations are only just beginning, so her intervention would not mean any substantial help. Italy therefore should remain at peace and merely give us proofs of her friendship.

This letter was clear and unequivocal. Hitler told us not to meddle in his affairs, and that he had no need of help to settle the problems of northern Europe, least of all help from a nation in such a state of military unpreparedness as Italy.

In telling me about this letter Mussolini said that in talks he had had with Hitler the latter had always shown himself to be against sending Germans to the south and Italians to the north. Hitler believed that the Mediterranean climate would lower the fighting capacity of the Germans and that the same thing would happen to Italians sent to fight in northern Europe.

The calmness with which Mussolini discussed all this

[1] 16 December 1939. (*Translator.*)

with me was purely superficial, because immediately afterwards he jumped up and said very angrily:

Hitler and Ribbentrop do not understand anything! What they are doing is an exact repetition of the mistake made by William and his Chancellor in 1914 when they believed that England and France would condone the violation of Belgium. Now Hitler refuses our help unless he asks for it, if things go wrong. The Germans are terrible as enemies and unbearable as friends. But if Hitler intends to proceed entirely on his own, that means that I recover my liberty of action. You must immediately prepare plans to strengthen the fortifications on the German frontier.

This conversation made a great impression on my mind. It seemed to me that the future of the country was not being decided by a conscientious examination of its real interests, but depended more or less on an agreement between the two Dictators. And the refusal of our support had, as an immediate reaction, Mussolini's order to me to study the establishment of a line of defence against our ally! I believed that Hitler's plan, in so far as it referred to the non-intervention of Italy, corresponded to the realities of the situation. He considered that the Polish question did not affect our interests, and that even if England and France declared war, it was still a question for northern Europe and no affair of ours. He was convinced that Germany could settle matters single-handed, and that Italy could best help by sending supplies as she was doing at the moment, and not by the intervention of our badly armed and ill-equipped forces.

I thought that instead of being angry at Hitler's decision Mussolini ought to have been delighted.

෴   ෴   ෴

The establishment of even closer relations between

Hitler and Mussolini led in 1939 to an alliance between
the two countries, which came to be called the Rome–
Berlin Axis. But this alliance was not the outcome of common political interests nor of an instinctive sympathy between the two nations: it was planned and imposed by
their two Dictators. I do not want here to try to examine
the feelings of the German people about this partnership,
but I can affirm, and millions of Italians will agree with
me, that it did not represent the feelings of the Italian
people. Not only were they averse to it, but they feared
that it would endanger the country. A generation was
still living which had fought the Germans bitterly for over
three years and the feelings of the greater number of these
ex-service men had not changed.

Mussolini, as he believed himself to be always right,
ought to have taken these facts into account. Further,
given our state of unpreparedness, he ought to have
realized how fortunate it was that Hitler's declaration
absolved him from any moral necessity of fighting, if
indeed he ever had any such scruples. Or to put it on a
more material plane, it seemed to me that he ought to have
felt that he had escaped very cheaply from the obligations
of the alliance he had formed. But here there arose the
question of the pride of Dictator Number One, who must
be the master of Dictator Number Two. That he had been
politely put on one side, as if of no importance, infuriated
Mussolini and obscured his judgement.

❧   ❧   ❧

Here I would like to make a short digression. The King
told me during a conversation which I had with him in
1943 in Brindisi that Mussolini had never informed him
of his intention to form an alliance with Hitler. It was
only when the agreement was concluded and signed that

Mussolini decided to notify the King. Now Article 5 of the Constitution reads: 'Executive power appertains exclusively to the King . . . he declares war, makes treaties of peace, alliance and commerce. . . .' His Majesty showed his very deep resentment at these proceedings and expressed to Mussolini his anger at such a violation of the Constitution. 'It was not possible to undo what had been done,' added the King, 'without causing serious difficulties.'

∾   ∾   ∾

Meanwhile our Military Attaché in Berlin informed us that the German plan of attack had been worked out in detail and that the Germans considered that Poland would be overrun in four weeks. The declaration of war on Poland was followed immediately by the French and British declarations of war on Germany and by a declaration of non-belligerency on the part of Italy. This state of non-belligerency was not recognized in international relations, but, given the very confused situation, no Power protested.

I am not concerned with the story of the German-Polish campaign. The result was what could have been foreseen. Notwithstanding the legendary courage of the Poles, the superiority of numbers and armament was overwhelming.

English intervention did not go beyond the declaration of war; there was not, nor could there have been, any active support. France made a timid and limited advance beyond the Maginot Line—an advance which certainly did nothing to weaken the German attack in the east. Towards the end of the campaign the Russians occupied Polish territory east of the Vistula, and an agreement was made between the Germans and the Russians for the partition of Poland. This agreement seemed then, and would have been had it lasted, a real success for German diplomacy. By this means Germany avoided having to fight on two fronts, and could turn west to face the menace of France and England with her rear secured.

Mussolini bowed to the logic of facts. Although he continued to point out to everyone the complete lack of political insight of the Germans, he was forced to admit the complete military preparedness of his ally, and the foresight and masterly handling of the military operations.

Italy lived through many anxious days. Public opinion, ignorant of the facts and kept in the dark by a press entirely subservient to the régime, believed that our country willingly or unwillingly would find itself involved. The declaration of non-belligerency by itself was not sufficient to give a feeling of peace and security. The Italian people would have preferred a frank declaration of neutrality, which would have prevented a change of policy. However, even non-belligerency was received with favour, for if it did not go far enough, it lessened the danger of being involved in the war.

CHAPTER II

Mussolini decides on Intervention

THE Polish campaign at an end, the larger part of the German army was transferred to the frontiers of France, Holland, and Belgium. Skirmishes between patrols relieved the monotony of the situation. Suddenly the German Army leapt forward, like a spring that is released, and the unopposed occupation of Denmark and the rapid campaign in Norway followed. Once again the superiority of the equipment and training of the German forces was obvious. The British fleet attacked the German convoys but could not prevent the landing of large numbers of the enemy in Norway.

In Italy the rearmament programme and the necessary financial measures had been agreed upon, and the production of armaments by a number of firms had begun.

Suddenly, without asking anyone's advice, Mussolini sold four destroyers to Sweden and in addition allowed other nations to buy the first anti-tank weapons turned out by our factories. Mussolini's reply to my very strongly expressed remonstrances about these sales, which inevitably postponed the date fixed for the completion of the rearmament programme, was that as Chief of the General Staff I could only see one aspect of the affair—the military aspect. He as Head of the Government had a general purview of the most urgent needs of the nation. At the moment it was absolutely essential to have foreign currency to buy the wheat which we had to have. He added that the date, 1943, as the moment for the completion of our programme was purely arbitrary, as he had already told me, and that no vital decision would be made until we were entirely ready.

❧   ❧   ❧

In February the usual meetings of the Supreme Defence Committee took place. Each of the Chiefs of Staff made a full report on the programmes which had been laid down and on the work undertaken by the different firms. But at this moment there was a scene which I must describe in detail. The Minister for Foreign Exchange and Currencies, Riccardi, after having made a lengthy statement on our holdings in foreign currencies, made a violent attack on the Chiefs of Staff who had just presented programmes impossible of realization. He ended by demanding a revision of the plans for rearmament to bring them into line with the real financial position.

I replied immediately, and could not conceal my anger. I said quite frankly that, while I appreciated the lucid and exhaustive explanation which he had given of our holdings in foreign currencies, I did not consider that he had either the capacity or the authority to express any opinion on military matters. The rearmament programme had been drawn up by experts under the political direction of the Head of the Government.

The discussion was cut short by Mussolini who was obviously embarrassed by having promised the necessary financial resources which the Minister now declared were not available. As frequently happened in similar crises, he assumed the mantle of a prophet and solemnly announced that everything must be done and possibly done more quickly than was anticipated because we 'must not desert history'.[1] This pronouncement, although I realized that

---

[1] A favourite catchword of Mussolini's. Nobody knew exactly what it meant. (*Translator.*)

it had been made merely to settle or at least stop the discussion, worried me very much and next morning I went to see him to ask for assurances that nothing had been changed in the programme laid down in the memorandum of April of the previous year. Mussolini declared that his programme would not be altered, unless circumstances beyond his control forced us into war.

Meanwhile, the two armies which were facing each other continued the skirmishes between the patrols without showing any sign of undertaking a general offensive.

Mussolini badgered the Ambassador and the Military Attaché in Berlin to find out something of the German plans and the date for the opening of operations. Although I told him that the Supreme Command would never reveal a secret of such importance to a third party, Mussolini continued to believe that he personally ought to be informed and was extremely annoyed at being kept in the dark.

Everybody knew that nothing long remained a secret in Rome, where the Fascist hierarchy and still more their wives and mistresses were proud to show their knowledge of such 'secrets'. It is certain that Hitler, who was of course kept informed of the state of affairs by the numerous German secret police in our capital, would not give away a secret which any high command would guard most jealously.

On 10 May the great German machine swung into action, crushing all resistance. Everything went down before it; Holland and Belgium capitulated, the British Army in Belgium after heavy losses was obliged to evacuate the country, and the entire northern wing of the French Army collapsed. It was the end of Holland and Belgium, and France was doomed, her gallant troops seeming to be stricken with paralysis. Mussolini believed that England would fall, and that was his fundamental mistake. He was seized as it were by a frenzy of desire not to be absent from the victor's banquet. There was no meeting of the Fascist Grand Council or of the Council of Ministers. He never told his henchmen of the decision he had taken.

On 26 May, having gone to see him on a matter of routine business, I met Marshal Balbo[1] in the waiting-room. He had come to Rome to discuss the unhappy state of affairs in Libya, both from the military point of view and from that of the civilian population, which was suffering from a lack of food.

Mussolini sent us a message to come in together; I had hardly crossed the threshold of the vast room which he occupied, than I realized that he had something of the greatest importance to say to us. He was standing behind his writing-table, his hands on his hips, looking intensely serious, almost solemn. He did not speak at once but silently transfixed us with his penetrating stare. What was he going to say? Suddenly I found that I had difficulty in breathing. Finally he decided to speak and then with an air of inspiration, he announced: 'I wish to tell you that yesterday I sent a messenger to Hitler with my written declaration that I do not intend to stand idly by with my hands in my pockets, and that after 5 June I am ready to declare war on England.'

We were dumbfounded and seemed to have lost the power of speech.

Mussolini opened his eyes very widely to show his surprise at the coldness with which we had received his news.

When I was able to speak I said:

Your Excellency, you know perfectly well that we are absolutely unprepared—you have received complete reports every week. We have about twenty divisions with 70 per cent.

[1] Governor and Commander-in-Chief in Libya. (*Translator.*)

of the necessary equipment and training; and about another twenty divisions with 50 per cent. We have no tanks. The Air Force, as you know from General Pricolo's reports, is grounded. This is to say nothing of stores—we have not even sufficient shirts for the army. In such a state of affairs how is it possible to declare war? Our colonies lack everything. Our merchant shipping is on the high seas.

Feeling absolutely desperate I added, 'It is suicide.'

Mussolini did not answer for a few minutes and then said quite calmly:

You were right about the situation in Ethiopia in 1935. It is evident that to-day you are too excited to judge the situation correctly. I assure you the war will be over in September, and that I need a few thousand dead so as to be able to attend the peace conference as a belligerent.

So ended this tragic colloquy. I went at once to the Ministry of Foreign Affairs to see whether Ciano, who was notoriously anti-German and opposed to the war, had any more information. He knew no more than I did and was very unhappy over Mussolini's decision. He kept on saying, 'Mussolini is absolutely mad.'

I went home.

Everyone knows that the Head of the Government had all the information about our rearmament programme both from the Supreme Defence Committee and from the weekly reports of the Chiefs of Staff. Too many people were involved for this to have been a secret. Nothing was concealed from Mussolini. If therefore he, without consulting anyone, decided to declare war, his was the sole responsibility.

But can some of that responsibility rest on me as his chief adviser in military matters?

My conscience is perfectly clear; I did all I could to stand by the decision taken in 1939: what else could I have done? Resigned? But that would not have altered the situation, for Mussolini would never have considered going back on his declaration to Hitler. Besides, to abandon my post at the very moment when war was declared would have been very unpopular in the country which had always trusted me. Remaining at my post, I could prevent the mistakes which Mussolini would make in his complete ignorance of military affairs.

This belief was so strong that it overrode all other considerations. And so with a spirit torn with the gloomiest presentiments I set out on the cruel road to my Calvary, which was also, alas, the Calvary of the whole nation.

On 29 May Mussolini held a meeting in his office of all the Chiefs of Staff and announced officially his decision (already communicated to Hitler) to declare war on some date after 5 June. He wished to explain the motives which lay behind this decision and as his speech was taken down in shorthand, I can summarize the essential points:

1. It is impossible for us to avoid war.
2. We cannot fight on the side of the Allies.
3. We can only fight on the side of the Germans.

It remains to decide on the date, which is the most difficult question to decide in the rhythm of a war. This date had been fixed for the spring of 1941 (evidently by him).

After the occupation of Norway and the overrunning of Denmark, I had advanced the date to the beginning of September 1940. Now after the conquest of Holland, the surrender of Belgium, the invasion of France, and the general situation which that has brought about, I have again advanced the date, and consider any day to be suitable after 5 June.

The situation does not allow of further postponement because otherwise we should run greater dangers than those which would have been caused by a premature intervention.

On the other hand, I have no doubt about the position of the Allies. In Hitler's last letter to me which I read to Marshal Badoglio yesterday,[1] he informed me that Germany had mobilized 220 divisions. Of these 10 are in Norway, 15 in Poland, and 25–30 are refitting. There remain 165, fully trained and armed, which Germany can throw into the fight whenever she pleases against 70–80 French divisions, while the English cannot now send reinforcements of any value. In addition, there is the crushing superiority of the German Air Force over that of the French; less overwhelming in the case of the English but still incontestably superior.

Can the situation be altered? No.

It cannot be changed by French production, for the Germans will bomb all the industrial centres, nor by American production for even if (in accordance with President Roosevelt's speech yesterday) America were to send her 2,500 existing planes, the transport to Europe would be a difficult undertaking. The Germans having occupied all the strategic points on the French coast, even their unloading would be problematical, at least on the north coast. Even the King of the Belgians has justified his action—and I think quite rightly—by pleading the terrible sufferings of his people. M. Pierlot is less important than the King, as he is a second-rate politician who acquired power by parliamentary methods. It is clear that the German strategy is directed to the capture of Paris and London. All our information gives the same description of the present situation and the only question is whether the army can hold the line of the French rivers.

I ask myself whether this resistance will not be broken when we intervene.

France cannot hope for anything before 1942, and by that time everything will be over.

If we wait for two weeks or a month, we shall not improve our military position, while we should give the Germans the impression that we were arriving after everything had been

[1] This was the answer to the letter from Mussolini announcing Italy's intervention. (*Translator.*)

finished, when there was no danger. There is the added consideration that we are not in the habit of hitting a man when he is down.

All this may be very important when it comes to making peace.

With regard to the attitude of the Italian people, which we must take into account, I would say this: up to 1 May they were afraid of going to war too soon, and were anxious to avoid such a contingency. That is understandable. Now they are agitated by two considerations:

1. The fear of arriving too late, so that our intervention would be valueless.
2. A certain feeling of emulation, a wish to show that they too can drop by parachute, attack tanks, &c.

This pleases me because it shows that the Italian people have stout hearts.

Such was Mussolini's understanding of the feelings of the Italian people.

CHAPTER III

At War

ON 4 June Mussolini obtained from the King the command of the armed forces in the field. This statement needs amplifying. I had often discussed with Mussolini the question of the conduct of the war. I had pointed out to him that the old formula, that at a given moment political action must cease and military action must take its place, had been proved to be out of date. Clemenceau in France and Lloyd George in England had both intervened in the conduct of the war; in fact, politics must always go on and could never be divorced from military action. That was what was happening at the moment; the heads of the Allied Governments were co-ordinating military operations, after consultation with their General Staffs.

In his speech to the Senate Mussolini declared that in the event of another war he would assume command of the armed forces. During the same sitting the title of Marshal of the Empire[1] was conferred on the King and on Mussolini. A few days afterwards I asked for an interview with the Crown Prince, explaining to him that I had not spoken directly to the King because it would have looked as if I were inspired by rancour at seeing a military rank given for a campaign which had been conducted under my command and for which I was solely responsible. I told the Prince that it was very dangerous to admit that Parliament could confer military rank; in allowing it to bestow the title of Marshal of the Empire on the King it had

---

[1] A higher rank than that of Marshal. (*Translator.*)

encroached on the royal prerogative. If such a principle were admitted, it meant that Parliament could also deprive officers of the rank they held. About the question of the command I made my ideas known to the Prince, who told me that he would convey them to the King. I heard nothing more, an indication that the King had sanctioned the proceedings. I therefore made no objection when Mussolini asked for the command of the forces in the field, after he had agreed to the condition that I must always approve every decision.

On 6 June Mussolini sent for me to say that an order of the day must be issued ordering all forces not in Italy to take up defensive positions. 'We will leave to others the responsibility of attacking us', he said. I pointed out that the responsibility rested on the first to declare war, and that what happened afterwards was the outcome of that initiative. The order was finally modified in the sense of prescribing that the Army should stand on the defensive, leaving the Navy and the Air Force to undertake an offensive after ten days, if a favourable opportunity presented itself.

I ought to add that our forces on the French frontier occupied purely defensive positions, which is proved by the fact that all our medium and heavy artillery and their shells were some distance from the front. Owing to the lack of roads it would have taken at least twenty-five days before our troops could have undertaken an offensive.

On 10 June Mussolini announced from the balcony of the Palazzo Venezia that Italy was at war. It was a pitiable spectacle. Herded like sheep between the officials and the riff-raff of the Fascist Party, the crowd had orders to applaud every word of the speech. But when it was over, the people dispersed of their own accord in complete silence. However much they were crushed under that iron system of coercion, they thoroughly understood the gravity of the situation and how terrible the consequences might be for the country.

Mussolini was exultant. He accepted with delight the most exaggerated compliments from the heads of the Party. I found myself in a corner of the room, feeling miserable. Ciano came up to me and said: 'Now it's done. There is no time for recriminations, only for action. Pray heaven we have good luck.'

I have no intention whatever of writing the history of our participation in the war during the few months that I continued to be Chief of the General Staff. History is written from documents and is almost always confined to a more or less accurate statement of facts. But the more important part, especially that which refers to the conversations, the arguments, and the disagreements between the principal actors, is necessarily omitted, because there is no written documentation. That is why official history is nearly always cold and lacks light and shade.

I will limit myself to certain essential points: the attack on France and the armistice; the appointment of Graziani to succeed Balbo; the opening of the campaign against Greece.

On 15 June Mussolini sent for me and ordered me to begin the attack on the French frontier on 18 June. I told him that in my view there were two reasons against this attack. The first was technical—our positions were purely defensive, as he knew, and it would take twenty-five days to go over to the offensive. The second was moral—the French army was disintegrating and the Germans had no need of our help to complete its destruction. We should not be affording useful or decisive support and we should cut a very poor figure, attacking a nation which was already beaten to the earth.

This was the second clash which I had with Mussolini; the first had been over the declaration of war.

After a few minutes' silence he said very gravely, picking his words carefully:

Marshal, as Chief of the General Staff you are my adviser on military but not on political questions. The attack on France, even in view of the objections you have raised, is essentially a political question for me to decide on my own responsibility. War to-day is not like a combat between two knights of the Middle Ages, nor is it like the battle of Fontenoy in which one side invited the other to fire first. To-day the objective is to annihilate the enemy, and every advantage must be seized to achieve that aim. For the rest, I do not intend to demand Savoy which is French, but Nice, Corsica, and Tunisia. If we limit our intervention merely to helping the collapse of France we shall have no right to our share of the booty. As to the disposition of our forces and the time needed to undertake an offensive, I consider that—given the condition of the French Army—it is not necessary to waste time in bringing up the artillery. I will give the necessary orders myself to the Army Chief of Staff.

As I was coming away from this painful interview, I met Ciano, the Foreign Minister. He saw from my face that something very serious had happened and said to me excitedly, 'He wants to kick a man who is down.' He had not time to say anything more for at that moment the Head of the Government sent for him.

The attack only penetrated the enemy's defences for a short distance but as a result of the bad weather and our lack of equipment, it caused us a considerable number of casualties, especially from frost-bite.

Meanwhile France had asked for an armistice and the German High Command sent us a copy of the terms they were imposing with the advice that we should do the same. But during the negotiations with the French delegates, among whom was my friend General Pariseau, I cancelled at their request the article which would have obliged them to send back to Italy all the Italian political refugees who were in their country. This seemed to me such an ignominious condition that I did not hesitate for a moment in making this decision. It earned me a bitter reproof from Mussolini. I tried in addition to accede to all the other requests of the French delegates.

We returned to Rome in the late evening and talking to the Italian representatives I said, 'I have never felt more uncomfortable and unhappy than I do at this moment.' As many of the Italian and French delegates will still be alive when these words are printed, they can testify to the truth of this statement.

Shortly afterwards I was one of the party which accompanied Mussolini when he made a tour of the western front. During a wait at a railway station in Piedmont we received a wireless message which informed us that Marshal Balbo had been killed in an aeroplane accident. He had arrived over Tobruk just after an enemy raid, his aeroplane was believed to be English, there was heavy anti-aircraft fire, and it crashed in flames.

Mussolini received the news without showing the slightest emotion; perhaps the disappearance of the only one of the Fascist hierarchy who had dared to challenge his supremacy was not altogether unwelcome. Anyhow, he made no comment and only asked me who should be appointed to succeed him.

I was not at all sure that Marshal Graziani was in the right place as Chief of Staff of the Army. He was lacking in the necessary experience and had no real understanding of the complex problems with which he was called upon to deal. But I thought him a good commander of troops in the field; he had given proof of his ability during the operations in Libya, and especially during the Abyssinian campaign, as general commanding on the southern front. He also possessed unrivalled knowledge of the Cyrenaican-Egyptian sector, having been Governor and General Commanding the troops in Cyrenaica during the last phase of the revolt of the Senussi. I did not hesitate therefore to propose him to Mussolini, who immediately agreed.

I must confess that I was completely mistaken. Perhaps as a result of the wounds he received at Addis Ababa during the attempt on his life by the Abyssinian national-ists, Marshal Graziani proved himself to be a very poor commander and so frightened for his own safety that he spent almost all his time in a shelter which he had fitted up as a residence in the suburbs of Cyrene. The truth of this statement is amply confirmed by the officers and men of the Libyan Expeditionary Force.

When the British offensive drove our troops back beyond Benghazi, Marshal Graziani sent Mussolini so despairing and hopeless a telegram that it was obvious that he had entirely lost control of the situation. In it he declared that his presence with the troops under his command, who were fighting desperately to hold up the enemy's advance, was quite useless. He proposed to Mussolini that he should retire to Tripoli (a thousand miles distant) to organize an armed camp there, leaving his junior officers to extricate themselves from the hopeless position in which they had been involved by the lack of judgement of their Commander-in-chief. Moreover, a little later, on the plea of ill health, he returned by air to Italy.

Mussolini, infuriated by such conduct, declared to the King that he would have Graziani court-martialled for cowardice for abandoning his post. The King pointed out that a general who in the past had shown courage and ability and who had held important commands, had better in the first instance be called before a court of inquiry. This was agreed to and the court was appointed, presided over by Admiral of the Fleet Di Revel, and after a searching investigation presented its report.

I have read this important document in which Graziani's conduct was exhaustively examined and the very gravest strictures were passed on his behaviour both as Commander-in-chief and as a soldier. This report was dated 28 February 1942, and I cannot understand how Mussolini, with such evidence in his possession, did not court-martial Graziani as he had originally intended to do.

This was the general whom Mussolini eventually chose to organize and command the troops of the neo-Fascist republic.

◦   ◦   ◦

Now I come to the campaign against Greece.

Ciano was the evil genius of this campaign. He considered the Albanian-Greek sector as his private sphere of influence. He had installed one of his creatures, Jacomoni, as Lieutenant-Governor of Albania and had loaded him with favours. Jacomoni's role was that of flatterer and mouth-piece of Ciano. Mussolini in his speech at the Adriano Theatre after the conquest of Greece (thanks to German intervention) declared that there was a document in existence which proved that the plan of campaign had been drawn up by the Chiefs of Staff of the armed forces and approved by him. This statement is inexact and incomplete. The question of Greece had never been raised. It is true that the neutrality of the Greek Government left much to be desired; British ships, both submarines and surface craft, were willingly repaired and hidden in the many inlets of the Greek mainland and the islands. According to Ciano, our Government had often called the attention of the Greek Government to its duty as a neutral, but the General Staff never envisaged these complaints as likely to lead to war.

The first hint that something was being plotted in this sector came in a remark which Mussolini made to me. 'Up to the present only the Navy has played any considerable part in the war, and in a subsidiary role, the Air Force. We must find something for the Army to do.' I pointed out that the Libyan sector was of exceptional importance to us, and that was the exclusive responsibility of the Army. But this did not satisfy Mussolini, and it was not till much later that he grasped that our essential problem was the Mediterranean.

At the beginning of October Mussolini ordered the General Staff to prepare a statement on the forces which would be needed in Albania for an attack on Greece.

The General Staff having drawn up a plan, General Roatta and I had an interview with Mussolini on 14 October to discuss it with him. We decided that if Bulgaria entered the war and drew off six to eight Greek divisions, we should need twenty divisions. It was also necessary to build up stocks of rations and munitions in view of the inadequate port facilities at Valona and Durazzo. A High Command and an Army Command would have to be set up.

The next day (15 October) Mussolini summoned a meeting at the Palazzo Venezia which was attended by Ciano, Jacomoni, General Visconti-Prasca, General Roatta the second-in-command of the Army Staff, Admiral Cavagnari the second-in-command of the Naval Staff, and General Pricolo the Under-Secretary and Chief of the Air Staff. Major Trombetti, an experienced shorthand-typist, acted as secretary and prepared a verbatim report.

Ciano opened the proceedings by giving an account of

his incessant protests against the unneutral behaviour of the Greek Government, who had denied allegations or distorted facts, proving that diplomatic notes by themselves would not bring about any change in the situation. He declared that Greek society was thoroughly corrupt, and that already he had enough support to ensure success. Jacomoni then spoke, declaring that all the Albanian patriots and troops were burning with the desire to liberate the Epirus once and for all, and that he was hardly able to prevent the Albanians from crossing the frontier. After him General Visconti-Prasca, evidently imbued with the same political ideas as Jacomoni, explained his plan: to advance with the forces at his disposal into the Epirus, protecting his flank by the occupation of the Pindus passes by battalions of Alpini. Arrived at Arta he could be reinforced for his advance on Athens by three more divisions which could be landed at that port.

I then pointed out that part of the Greek army was stationed on the Bulgarian frontier and it was essential to know what would be the attitude of that country. If it remained neutral the Greek army might seriously menace our left wing towards Koritza. Mussolini said that he would immediately write a personal letter to King Boris pointing out that if Bulgaria wished to have an outlet to the Aegean, this was a favourable moment to obtain it. He agreed that while waiting for an answer from King Boris, the Visconti-Prasca plan should be examined in detail by the Army General Staff.

This examination was carried out and it was agreed that it was likely to succeed if all the conditions described by Ciano and Jacomoni really existed.

A few days later Admiral Cavagnari came to tell me that the canal leading to Arta had been blocked and that in consequence it would be impossible to send the divisions

by sea to that port. As Mussolini was temporarily away
from Rome, I at once went to Ciano to tell him of Cavagnari's report. Ciano was very much annoyed and begged
me to find out from the Navy if the news was really true.
He then told me that he had succeeded in getting the support of several leading Greeks, some of whom were actually
in the Government, who were prepared to turn out the
Government and join the Axis. He added that the cost had
been rather high, but that the success justified the outlay.
Furthermore, an understanding had been arrived at with
the troops in the Epirus and he had appointed Pariani, who
was in Albania, to organize rest centres and to provide food
for these troops.

This is the real story of what happened. King Boris replied that although he thoroughly understood the advantage of collaborating with Italy, public opinion in his
country was such that for the present he could not do
anything. Handing me the letter Mussolini exclaimed
with contempt: 'These chicken-livered kings never succeed
in taking any action! We'll do without him. Prasca's
march will be so rapid that it will draw off the Greek
forces in the north, even if they don't disintegrate by every
man going home.'

I was not satisfied and insisted that another division
should be sent to strengthen our flank on the Koritza
front; this saved us from disaster. The campaign began
and its outcome is known to everyone.

Far from making common cause with us the Greek
troops in the Epirus fought bravely on the Kalamas
Mountains. On the other hand, the Albanians proved
themselves treacherous allies, committing acts of sabotage
or joining the Greeks. It was necessary to withdraw and
disarm some of them.

On 10 November Mussolini summoned a conference of

myself, Cavagnari, Pricolo, Roatta, and Sorice, with Major
Trombetti as secretary. He began with the remark that
events had proved that the political forecasts of Jacomoni
and the military forecasts of General Visconti-Prasca were
absolutely unfounded. Therefore it was necessary to
examine the position calmly and objectively and to consider measures to restore it.

As I was extremely anxious to make it quite clear who
was responsible, I replied:

At the meeting on 14 October you asked me and Roatta how
many troops were needed for an attack on Greece. As a result
of the studies of the General Staff of the Army, General Roatta
declared that if Bulgaria also attacked Greece, we should need
twenty divisions. The dispatch of another ten divisions with
a commander-in-chief and an Army commander was discussed.
On 15 October there was another meeting at which Count
Ciano, General Soddù, Lieutenant-Governor Jacomoni and
Visconti-Prasca were present. As a result of the statements of
Ciano and Visconti-Prasca, you decided to attack on 26 October, a date which was subsequently changed to 28 October.
We tried to make all possible preparations during this time.

I have reviewed these facts to show that neither the General
Staff nor the Army Staff had anything to do with the plans that
were adopted, which were entirely contrary to our method of
procedure. This method is based on the principle of thorough
preparation before action is taken.

(This statement was deleted from the verbatim report
of Major Trombetti, a copy of which was sent to me as
Chief of the General Staff.)

The number and character of the reinforcements to be
sent was then decided, but notwithstanding the hurried
dispatch of these troops the situation remained very grave.

At the end of November Mussolini summoned me and
General Roatta and expressed bitter regret that General

Visconti-Prasca's plan had been accepted. At this I could
not restrain myself and I said:

You are in command. Two plans were presented to you,
one by General Prasca based on the political conditions which
Ciano and Jacomoni declared to exist; the second prepared by
the General Staff of the Army which was based on the assumption that Bulgaria would enter the war. You chose Visconti-
Prasca's plan. It does not seem to me, therefore, that any blame
attaches to the General Staff of the Army.

Mussolini said nothing and dismissed us. As we came
away General Roatta thanked me very warmly for my
defence of the General Staff of the Army.

The next day Colonel Sorice, Head of the War Cabinet,
told me that Mussolini was very angry with me for what
I had said in front of General Roatta. A few days later an
attack on the General Staff appeared in the Cremona
paper edited by Farinacci.[1]

I went to Mussolini to ask that he should contradict
what Farinacci had said, to which he replied that Farinacci
detested me and was solely responsible for the article but
that he had sent for Farinacci to discuss the matter. I
realized at once that Mussolini, who, when it came to the
point, was afraid of responsibility, was casting the blame
on his jackal. I asked for four days' leave during which he
and I would consider our future relations. When I saw
Mussolini again he told me that he had decided to appoint
General Cavallero to succeed me.

There was a very unpleasant scene. Having tried to
hold me responsible for the acceptance of Visconti-Prasca's
plan, I told him that a commander was always held to
account for any mistake; but in this specific instance he had

---

[1] *La Regime Fascista.* Farinacci was a former Secretary of the Fascist Party,
notorious for his anti-clerical and anti-Jewish activities, and the leader of the
pro-German faction of the Fascist hierarchy. (*Translator.*)

not had the courage to accept the responsibility for his own
decision and that he wanted a scapegoat. I also told him
that I had no intention of collaborating in any way with
him in the future and withdrew. On the following day the
Federal Secretaries of the Fascist Party all over Italy,
started a violent campaign against me and the personal
insults with which they assailed me were unbelievable.

I asked for an interview with the Head of the Government and demanded an explanation. He declared that
Serena, the Secretary to the Party, was to blame, and that
he personally disapproved and had already put a stop to
the attacks. These were his usual tactics. I replied that
Serena was too stupid and frightened to take such a step
by himself; it was of little use to say that So-and-so was
responsible when I knew that not one of his followers
would dare to act without his approval. With these words
I rose and went away. I never saw Mussolini again.

There are two other matters with which I must deal
before closing this miserable chapter.

In November I went to Innsbruck to meet the Chief of
the German General Staff, General Keitel. He immediately said to me that we had begun the offensive against
Greece without informing the German General Staff and
that the Führer had not intended to upset the situation
in the Balkans because Germany received considerable
supplies from Greece which she might feel the lack of in
the future. 'If', said Keitel, 'I had been warned, I would
have flown to Rome to prevent the attack.'

I was obliged to tell him the truth, which was that we
had received orders from Mussolini to say nothing to the
Germans. When I had objected that we were bound to
inform them under the terms of the Alliance, he had

answered angrily: 'Did they tell us about the campaign in Norway? Did they tell us about the opening of the offensive on the western front? They behaved as if we did not exist—I shall repay them in their own coin.'

◇   ◇   ◇

Ever since the days of Balbo, Headquarters in Libya had been asking for a supply of tanks. I had sent all that we had in Italy—seventy-four Marks 11 and 13.

Mussolini had charged me to ask Keitel for a large proportion of the seven hundred tanks which the Germans said they had captured from the French, but to refuse an offer of an armoured division. 'If they get a footing in the country, we shall never be rid of them,' he said. Keitel refused to give us the French tanks saying that they were in need of considerable repairs. He offered instead two armoured divisions, which, in accordance with Mussolini's orders, I had very reluctantly to refuse.

In April 1943 I met in Rome General von Rintelen, the German Military Attaché with our High Command, and he told me that both Keitel and he had been astounded at my refusal of two armoured divisions which they knew Italy needed badly and which were accepted later. I explained to him that I had explicit orders from Mussolini to refuse them.

CHAPTER IV

The Dictatorship 'in extremis'

Having given up my post as Chief of the General Staff I spent my time at home but I never ceased to attend the meetings of the Senate and I used to go to my clubs. Two years passed, marked by continual anxiety for the fate of the country and by deaths in my family. The people seemed completely apathetic, drugged by the anaesthetic with which they had been doped for twenty years, and they only awoke slowly to the gravity of the situation.

But three military events tore aside the bandage with which the Fascist authorities endeavoured to blind the eyes of the Italian people. Consternation and anger spread through the country and hatred of the Government was unbounded.

It was fanned by our disasters in North Africa. The fortunate counter-offensive of Rommel had carried the Italo-German forces as far as El Alamein; Mussolini, who never missed a chance for self-glorification, went to Cyrenaica, taking with him an Arab horse and the sword of Islam, so as to be ready for a triumphal entry into Alexandria. But after some probing of the front Rommel convinced himself that the English resistance was not to be overcome. So he retreated and organized a defensive line at Sollum where he established himself. History will reveal who gave the order to hold on at El Alamein when every day it became more and more difficult to bring up supplies, and the enemy was being continually reinforced. This was a fundamental mistake and rumour attributes it to Hitler. The consequences were inevitable.

The British counter-offensive, launched with enormous

D

resources, overwhelmed the Italians and the Germans.
Meanwhile, British and American forces had landed in
North Africa and our troops, after a terrible retreat to
Tunisia, were caught in a pincer movement and com-
pelled to surrender at Tunis.

The second catastrophe was in Russia. In that distant
theatre of operations we had at first an army corps; then
at the very moment when troops were urgently needed in
the Mediterranean theatre, the army corps was reinforced
until it amounted to an army. Incredible as it may seem,
our magnificent Alpine troops were sent to fight on the
plains of Russia. When the Soviet offensive overran the
German, Roumanian, and Italian positions, three-quarters
of our army was lost. As at El Alamein, the Germans
seized all our means of transport to facilitate their own
retreat, leaving the Italian troops to face a hopeless situation. The news of such inhuman behaviour spread all over
Italy and made a profound impression.

The third on the list of these military disasters were the
air attacks on Turin, Milan, and Genoa. Our anti-aircraft
defences were deplorably inefficient, fighter aircraft were
practically non-existent, there were no shelters and no
preparations for dealing with fires, and no plans had been
made for the evacuation of the civil population who consequently fled in confusion. Commenting on this in the
Chamber Mussolini declared that he had given orders
some time ago for the cities to be evacuated—as if this did
not need organization by the authorities and was merely
to be left to private initiative. The people realized that
no steps had been taken to deal with such attacks and that
if the war went on all our towns and means of communication would be destroyed.

Conscious of our complete helplessness, the morale of
the people rapidly deteriorated; in trains, in trams, in

the streets, wherever they were, they openly demanded peace and cursed Mussolini. Anger with the Fascist régime was widespread, and everywhere one heard: 'It does not matter if we lose the war because it will mean the end of Fascism.'

            ⟨◇⟩   ⟨◇⟩   ⟨◇⟩

I never saw the King after I relinquished my appointment as Chief of the General Staff on 6 December 1940. During the early months of 1943 many of my friends begged me to go to him to acquaint him with the real state of the country and to induce him to bring about a change in the internal situation. On principle I was entirely opposed to such action. It seemed to me that the King was the best judge as to whether he considered it advisable to consult a Marshal of Italy who had played a considerable part in the 1915–18 war, and who after pacifying Libya had conquered an empire for him. But as their pressure on me continued, I asked for and obtained an audience which took place at the Quirinal. The King listened to my lengthy exposition and my rather radical suggestions, but he did not make any comment.

The person who was eagerly seeking a way out of the impasse was the Crown Princess. I had a talk with her in the neighbourhood of Cogne, having taken the utmost care that news of our meeting should not leak out. The Princess, with her quick intelligence, showed a complete understanding of the state of affairs and urged me to take drastic measures. We had many talks in Rome, always with the same precautions because of the surveillance under which I was kept. The subject of our discussions was always the same, but the difficulties appeared insurmountable: how could I, without any organization behind me, overthrow the Government?

I got into touch with the Minister to the Royal Household who had been my ordnance officer for some months
when I was a lieutenant. The Duke Acquarone told me
that the King had already decided on a change of government, and he put me in touch with General Ambrosio, the
Chief of the General Staff, a brave, capable, and honest
officer. I am very glad to be able to pay a tribute to his
work and to express my warm friendship for him. We
examined the situation together and were convinced that
it was no longer possible to postpone taking action. We
agreed that there were two objectives to be achieved as
rapidly as might be—the arrest of Mussolini and half
a dozen leading Fascists, and the neutralization of the
Fascist Militia, especially the armoured division which
was in the neighbourhood of Rome.

Ambrosio thought that it would take a month to collect
the necessary forces in Rome without arousing suspicion.
This discussion took place at my house in the presence of
Duke Acquarone who undertook to inform the King.

At the end of June I had talks with Bonomi,[1] Casati,[2]
and Bergamini[3] so that I should be sure of a Ministry
which would unite the leaders of the different political
parties. We discussed the political action to be taken
immediately after the disappearance of Mussolini, but one
problem seemed to be insoluble—how to free ourselves
from the German stranglehold and declare an armistice.
I could have got into touch with British representatives in
Switzerland through confidential agents, but they could
have given no guarantees, and the only outcome would

[1] Ivanoe Bonomi, Minister of Public Works under Orlando; Minister of
War under Nitti; Minister of Finance under Giolitti. Former Reformist,
Socialist. (*Translator*.)

[2] Senator Alessandro Casati, Liberal. (*Translator*.)

[3] Senator Alberto Bergamini, founded and directed *Il Giornale d'Italia*,
1901–24. Right-wing Liberal. (*Translator*.)

have been to inform the British Government that I wished
to come to an understanding with them at all costs.

Meanwhile, the Allies had landed in Sicily; but before
this took place heavy air attacks had destroyed all the railway lines between Salerno and Foggia, making the sending
of supplies extremely difficult. As soon as Mussolini was
informed of the Allied preparations for a landing he
made a speech, perhaps the stupidest of his career, in
which he declared that when the enemy landed on the
beaches they would be annihilated by our fire. As a
matter of fact they had very little difficulty in landing
owing to the poor state of the defences of the island, and
were able at once to isolate and then occupy the whole of
the western sector of Sicily.

About 15 July General Ambrosio came to tell me that
on 18 July there was to be a meeting at Feltre between
Mussolini and Hitler which he, Bastianini (the Under-
Secretary for Foreign Affairs), and Alfieri (the Ambassador
in Berlin) were to attend. He said that when the Germans
had refused our request for military help, he had told
Mussolini that the position was desperate and it was
essential that the Head of the Government should have a
complete 'show down' with Hitler so as to make him
realize that Italy was no longer able to continue the war.
Ambrosio added that he had very little hope that Mussolini
would take his advice but he was convinced that it was
absolutely necessary.

At the meeting on 19 July Hitler talked for two hours
on how badly our aerodromes were protected, and said
that he did not wish to send any more planes to be
destroyed on the ground. It was obviously an excuse for
most of our airfields had been in German hands for some
time, and therefore they were responsible.

Mussolini did not open his mouth, and that was the end

of the meeting. But as he was to spend some time with Hitler in the train and the motor-car on the way back to the airfield, Ambrosio, Bastianini, and Alfieri all protested most strongly, and said that he must tell Hitler that Italy could not go on fighting. 'Perhaps you think I'm frightened of him?' answered Mussolini. But all the same he did not have the courage to tell Hitler what was essential for the salvation of his country.

On the morning of 20 July Mussolini returned to Rome and that evening sent for General Ambrosio. He said that after having thought it over he had decided to write a letter to Hitler in which he would say frankly that Italy must give up the struggle. General Ambrosio retorted that this ought to have been said at Feltre, that the letter—if it were ever written—like so many others dealing with matters of the greatest importance, would remain unanswered. As his protests had been ignored, he did not wish to share the responsibility and therefore resigned his post as Chief of the General Staff.[1] Even this step, which perhaps might have made the name of Mussolini less hated, was not taken—the letter was never written.

On the day of this meeting about 500 Allied bombers made a heavy attack on the railway stations in Rome and on the aerodromes round the capital, doing great damage to the crowded quarters near them. I went immediately to visit the worst of the destruction, and the crowd shouted to me 'Save what can be saved!' Poor people, far worse sufferings were in store for them.

[1] His resignation was not accepted. (*Translator.*)

CHAPTER V

The 'Coup d'état'

DISORDERS and attempts to evade responsibility were increasing within the Fascist Party. Ciano, the former favourite of Mussolini and his successor *in pectore*, had rebelled more or less openly and been deposed from his position as Foreign Minister and been made Ambassador to the Holy See.[1] Grandi,[2] one of the best-known members of the Party, had for some time retired into the background. He had been deprived of the Ministry of Justice but had not been able to escape altogether (as he certainly wanted to do) and remained President of the Chamber of Fasces and Corporations. Bottai,[3] who was still Minister for Education, had tried vainly to get into touch with me again; he had now nothing to do and was an open 'frondist'. It was common knowledge that Cini,[4] an industrial magnate, who against his will had been made Minister of Communications, had spoken with great frankness and firmness on the impossible situation in which the country found itself. He had pointed out the necessity for a complete change of policy and had, in addition, tendered his resignation, which had not been accepted.

Mussolini at this time had a recurrence of his duodenal ulcer trouble, but his illness was deliberately exaggerated

[1] 7 February 1943. (*Translator.*)

[2] Count Dino Grandi, Minister of Foreign Affairs, 1929–32; Ambassador in London, 1932–9; Minister of Justice, 1939 to 5 February 1943; President of the Chamber, November 1939 to July 1943. (*Translator.*)

[3] Minister of Corporations, 1929–32; Governor of Rome, 1935; Minister of Education, 1936 to 5 February 1943. (*Translator.*)

[4] Senator Vittorio Cini, President of the Società Adriatica di Elettricità. (*Translator.*)

in order to prove that he was no longer in a fit state to govern the country. In fact the old proverb was once again to be proved true: the rats were leaving the sinking ship.

On the morning of 24 July a rumour spread through Rome that the members of the Fascist Grand Council had insisted that Mussolini should summon a meeting of the Council for that evening. The news was, however, received with considerable incredulity. There was talk of a plot by leading Fascists against the Duce, and it was even thought possible that it might lead to violence. As a matter of fact the Council met and the discussion continued to a very late hour.

The next morning, Sunday, 25 July, there was the sensational news that the Fascist Grand Council had demanded Mussolini's resignation. It was said that his most bitter assailants had been Ciano, Grandi, De Bono,[1] and Bottai. The proceedings were summed up in a resolution.[2] The

[1] Senator Emilio de Bono, Quadrumvir of March on Rome; Senator, 1923; Governor of Tripolitania, 1925–8; Minister of the Colonies, 1929; High Commissioner of East Africa, January 1935; Commander-in-Chief, April 1935; shot by neo-Fascists after a trial at Verona, 1944. (*Translator.*)

[2] This was the original text of the resolution:

'The Fascist Grand Council, meeting in this supreme hour of danger, first salutes the heroic combatants in every arm who, side by side with the noble Sicilians in whom burns the united faith of the Italian people, are upholding the historic tradition of courage and the indomitable spirit of sacrifice of our glorious armed forces.

'The Fascist Grand Council having examined the internal and the international situation and the political and military conduct of the war: Proclaims the sacred duty of all Italians to defend at all costs the unity, independence and liberty of the country which are the fruits of the sacrifices of four generations from the Risorgimento till today, and also to defend the lives and future of the Italian people: Affirms the necessity for the spiritual and material union of all Italians in this grave and decisive moment in the fortunes of the nation: Declares that with this aim in view the immediate restoration of all the organs of state is essential, so that the Crown, the Grand Council, the Government, Parliament and the Corporations may

excitement in the city was intense; violent arguments led to brawls in the streets, Fascists being roughly handled.

In the afternoon some intimate friends came to see me. At about five o'clock the Minister of the Royal Household arrived to say that the King wished to see me urgently.

While I was changing into uniform the Minister hurriedly told me that Mussolini had gone to see His Majesty to inform him of the result of the meeting of the Grand Council. The King had forced him to resign and as he left the palace he had been arrested and taken to a Carabinieri[1] barracks. The King wished me to become Head of the Government. Very much disturbed by such serious news, I went to the Villa Savoia.[2]

The King was quite calm and told me at once what had happened. What he said made so deep an impression on me that I can repeat it almost word for word.

This morning Mussolini asked me for an interview which I fixed for this afternoon at 4 p.m. at this villa. When he arrived Mussolini told me that a meeting of the Fascist Grand Council had been held and had passed a vote of censure on him, but

carry on the tasks and responsibilities assigned to them under the constitution and the laws:

'Invites the Government to beg the King, to whom the whole nation looks with loyalty and confidence, that he should for the honour and safety of the country, assume the effective command of the Army, Navy and Air Force according to article 5 of the Constitution, and take the supreme initiative of command which our institutions confer upon him and which has been throughout our history the glorious heritage of the House of Savoy.'

This resolution was signed by: De Bono, De Vecchi, Grandi, De Marsico, Acerbo, Federzoni, Balella, Gottardi, Bignardi, De Stefani, Bottai, Rossoni, Marinelli, Alfieri, Ciano, Bastianini.

Seven voted against it: Biggini, Polverelli, Tringali, Frattari, Scorza, Buffarini, Balbiati.

Farinacci presented a resolution of his own which, however, was not voted on. Suardo abstained from voting.

[1] Semi-military police force, responsible for the maintenance of law and order all over the country. (*Translator*.)

[2] The Royal Residence on the outskirts of Rome. (*Translator*.)

he believed that this resolution was not in order. I replied at once that I did not agree with him; the Grand Council was an organ of State which he himself had created by means of a law which had been passed by the Chamber and the Senate; therefore every decision of the Grand Council was valid. 'Then according to Your Majesty I ought to resign,' he said with considerable violence. 'Yes,' I answered, and told him that I forthwith accepted his resignation.

His Majesty added,

When he heard this Mussolini collapsed as if he had had a blow over the heart. 'Then my ruin is complete,' he muttered hoarsely.

Having taken leave of His Majesty, Mussolini went out and not seeing his car, he asked an officer where it had gone. 'It is standing in the shade at the side of the Villa,' the officer answered. Mussolini went in the direction indicated when suddenly he found himself surrounded by secret police who asked him to get into a motor ambulance which was standing a little distance away. 'Can't I use my car?' he asked, 'And where are you taking me?' 'To a place where you will be quite safe,' answered the officer. Without saying anything more, Mussolini got into the motor ambulance and was taken to a Carabinieri barracks.

The King then asked me to become Head of the Government; I knew that the country trusted me, that His Majesty would be embarrassed if I refused, and that my refusal would still further complicate a situation which called for immediate action. I put all personal considerations on one side and faced the terrible responsibility I was undertaking. I answered, 'I am very conscious of my lack of political experience; I have never taken any part in politics, but I understand the pressing needs of the moment and I accept. As for my colleagues in the Ministry, I have here a list of the politicians who have promised to

collaborate and of the parties they represent.' I read to
His Majesty the names of Bonomi as Minister of Internal
Affairs, Casati as Minister of Education, of Soleri,[1] of
Bergamini, of Einaudi,[2] and others.

The King was entirely opposed to this plan. He said
that I would have to act with great rapidity and energy
both internally and in our relations with the Germans,
and that I must not be surrounded by politicians.

'You must have a Ministry of experts', he added, 'who will
carry out your orders efficiently.' 'But as a result', I said, 'I
shall be entirely cut off from public opinion and shall have no
contact with the feeling of the country.' 'No,' said the King,
'the whole country is with you and will follow you. I am sure
that your political friends will support you even if they are not
in the Ministry. Here is a list of the new Ministers; they are
all experienced and capable officials, with whom you can work.'

So, as the King was determined to have his own way,
I ended by agreeing.

It was decided that in view of our precarious position,
it was not possible to announce that Italy would ask for
peace. Such a step would undoubtedly have provoked
an immediate and violent German reaction, which the
Government (not yet in existence) could not have faced.

The King showed me two proclamations already printed,
which he and I (as Head of the Government) would issue.
I learned afterwards that Signor Orlando[3] had helped in
drawing up these proclamations in which it was announced
that the war would go on.

[1] Senator Marcello Soleri, Minister of Finance, 1921; Justice, 1922.
Liberal. (*Translator.*)

[2] Professor Luigi Einaudi, well-known economist. Liberal. (*Translator.*)

[3] Senator Vittorio Orlando, Prime Minister 1917–19; Italian Delegate
Peace Conference in Paris, 1919. Liberal. (*Translator.*)

As soon as this was over I went back to my house where an enormous and delirious crowd made it difficult for me to get in.

At two o'clock in the morning I was summoned to the Ministry of War, where a crisis had arisen. General Galbiati, Chief of Staff of the Fascist Militia, had apparently decided to resist. But my very peremptory order to place himself under the command of my trusted friend General Armellini, whom I had appointed to command the Militia, had the desired effect. Galbiati resigned and did not take any action.

I wrote at once to Mussolini assuring him that he need not fear for his personal safety, that his arrest and confinement had been necessary to save him from the fury of the people who otherwise would most certainly have attacked him. Mussolini sent me a scrap of paper on which was a message which he had dictated to the officer who had taken my letter, and which he signed. In this he declared that he was very pleased that we had decided to go on fighting and thanked me warmly for having secured his safety.

Cheering crowds paraded the streets of Rome all night long. There was occasional firing and many Fascist headquarters were attacked and sacked.

So ended this historic day.

◦   ◦   ◦

There are three matters about which I wish to say something more.

First of all the arrest of Mussolini. As I have already explained, I had discussed with General Ambrosio the necessity for Mussolini's arrest, and as he was in command of the Army he undertook to carry this out. But as it happened we were by-passed; the arrest was both planned

and carried out by the Minister to the Royal Household
with the co-operation of the General Commanding the
Carabinieri: they had, of course, obtained the King's consent.[1]

The second matter I only heard about later from one
of the actors. This was the plan which had been agreed
upon by the leading Fascists for the summoning of the
Grand Fascist Council and for the vote against Mussolini.
It had been worked out at a series of meetings held during
the first two weeks of July. These conspirators did not
intend that the Party should abandon the reins of Government, and had therefore chosen three members of the
Council to form a triumvirate and assume power. Mussolini's position was not very clearly envisaged; some of them
wanted him to disappear altogether, others proposed that
he should be given some post but without any power. As
for the triumvirate (a reduced edition of the 'Quadrumvirate'),[2] the names I was given were those of Ciano,
Grandi, and Federzoni.[3] Later on I was given other names
and I am now uncertain which list was correct.

The triumvirate proposed, as shown by the resolution
presented to the Grand Council, that the King should
resume command of the armed forces, and that all organs
of the State should be restored. As I have said, events
moved too quickly both for them and for me.

But the Fascist leaders were convinced that without
Mussolini they could continue to run the country—which

[1] In his book *Come Firmai l'Armistizio di Cassibile*, General Castellano gives
a different account of the plot, which he organized under the direction of
Ambrosio. See 'I Signed the Italian Armistice', *New English Review*, September 1946, summary by Muriel Currey.

[2] A reference to the Quadrumvirate who organized the Fascist 'March on
Rome', 1922. (*Translator.*)

[3] Formerly leader of the Nationalist Party, which joined the Fascist
Party in 1924, for many years President of the Chamber. (*Translator.*)

shows how completely out of touch they were with public opinion, which was now expressing itself clearly and forcibly. They behaved as if they were completely deaf and were consequently cut off from all contact with the people. The King struck one resolute blow at their leader, and without any resistance or violence the whole Fascist structure collapsed. On 26 July one did not see a single person in Rome wearing the Fascist badge. Fascism fell, as was fitting, like a rotten pear.

The third matter about which I wish to say something was the failure of the King to abdicate.

In the discussions I had had with the Minister of the Royal Household, I had explained to him that not only in Lombardy but even in Piedmont[1] the people blamed the King for the continuance of the Fascist Party in power for so many years, and also for the present tragic situation. It seemed to me that, even if he acted with the greatest determination and showed that he realized that the path he had taken had led to disaster, he should recognize that he was partly responsible, and like Charles Albert after Novara, should abdicate in favour of Prince Umberto. I felt that his disappearance would strengthen and not weaken the monarchy.

But the Minister was entirely opposed to such a policy, and said that it was obvious that only the King could deal with a situation so fraught with unknown dangers as a change of government, because he alone had the experience and the energy. Prince Umberto had not been allowed to take any part in public affairs and would probably be completely bewildered. The Minister also assured me that the politicians had already discussed the question with the King who had absolutely refused to abdicate.

[1] Part of the patrimony of the House of Savoy and famous for its loyalty. (*Translator.*)

'If you take up this matter,' he added, 'you will fail, as the King is determined to remain at his post. The only result will be a coldness in your relations with His Majesty which will certainly not ease the task of the Government.'

So, convinced that any action on my part would be quite useless, I did not mention the matter to the King.

CHAPTER VI

A Review of the Situation

I EXPLAINED in the last chapter that both the King and I thought it impossible for Italy to withdraw from the struggle immediately. As this decision has given rise to many criticisms, I think it is essential to give our reasons.

During my talks with General Ambrosio, Chief of the General Staff, before the *coup d'état*, he gave me the latest information on our military situation of which I knew very little, for I was entirely dependent on newspaper reports. This situation was absolutely deplorable as the result both of our defeats and of the dispersal of our forces by Mussolini. All our resources in men and materials, which had been poured into the colonies, had disappeared; Libya had engulfed almost all our scanty reserves. In Russia, whither we had sent an entire army, we had lost two-thirds of the men and practically all the equipment. The Air Force had been almost wiped out in Libya. Most of our mercantile marine had been lost, and the Navy had suffered severely both in cruisers and destroyers. As the result of Mussolini's megalomania thirty-six divisions had been sent to France, Croatia, Montenegro, Albania, and Greece.

To defend the entire peninsula there were only twelve weak divisions, of which one was a much-depleted armoured division composed of the Fascist Militia. There were artillery divisions manning the coastal defences without artillery, with very few arms and with no transport. These represented an unfortunate creation of no practical value. Our forces were divided into three commands: one in the valley of the Po, another between Florence and Rome, and a third in Apulia, Basilicata, and Calabria.

General Ambrosio said that as a result of air attacks on our railway system, it was impossible to concentrate our forces. Motor transport was out of the question as our supply of vehicles had been reduced almost to nothing as a result of the losses in Libya.

The Germans had eight divisions in Italy of which four were heavily armoured, all being well supplied with motor transport which made a concentration easy. While we possessed about four hundred planes, the Germans had over eight hundred. In addition, in the Innsbruck zone there were large numbers of German troops so that eight divisions could be dispatched to Italy from various sectors at a few days' notice. This information was proved to be entirely correct as was shown by events after 26 July.

Given all these circumstances, a unilateral declaration by Italy of her intention to make peace would have meant handing ourselves over to the Germans bound hand and foot. It is only necessary to remember what happened in Roumania. According to their present Government, they had been conducting negotiations to free themselves from the Germans for some time, but they could only do so when the Russian armies were in a position to give immediate and substantial support.

I repeat, with absolute conviction, that an Italian declaration of a cessation of hostilities could only have resulted in the immediate occupation of the whole peninsula by the Germans, the overthrow of the Government, the creation of a Nazi–Fascist régime, and no assurance that the Allied Powers would distinguish between the Italian people and the Fascist Party.

◈   ◈   ◈

All these considerations had to be calmly weighed by those who had the tremendous responsibility of deciding

E

on a line of action, but the overwhelming tragedy of the situation was not understood by the mass of the people. Throughout the country, mingled with misery, bitterness, and grief there was a conviction which was summed up in the catch phrase—'Mussolini stands for war, Badoglio stands for peace.' It is useless to examine how such a simple idea came to dominate people's minds, but it is undeniable that it was believed by all sections of the community, educated and uneducated alike. How peace could be achieved was never considered, nobody stopped to consider; people did not argue about it; they took it for granted.

I was overwhelmed with letters and telegrams; votes of organizations and of communes all expressing the same desire. They did not stop to think how we were to free ourselves from the Germans and to open negotations with the Allies. It was the business of the Government to do both immediately. The first disillusionment that the people suffered was the issuing of the two proclamations by the King and myself stating that the war would continue. No one understood the imperative necessity for this action.

This disappointment, which led to an immediate re-action, was fomented by the propaganda of the B.B.C., especially in the speeches of Colonel Stevens, who had a large audience in Italy. I do not want to express my personal opinion on this line of policy of the Allies, but will content myself with the following extract from an article by George Glasgow which appeared in the *Contemporary Review* for October 1943.

Confronted with the fall of Mussolini, what was the attitude of the United Nations . . . they went on woodenly talking of unconditional surrender, and bombed Rome again. Was it not really understood in London and Washington that Italy at that time could not surrender because the country was under the control of the German military? In fact, if Italy had surrendered, it would have been an unconditional surrender to Hitler.[1]

But the people did not stop to reason, and strikes which had the most deplorable results broke out, especially in the north.

I remember that Signors Bonomi, Casati, Buozzi, Roveda, and others came to me with a resolution in which all the parties they represented demanded an immediate peace. I told them that peace was my chief and overwhelming desire, but I begged them to consider the enormous difficulties to be overcome. 'It is very hard to conclude a peace *à deux* and we have to do it *à trois*.'

⁕   ⁕   ⁕

Another belief very widely held, especially among the poorer classes, was that with the fall of Fascism all the difficulties of rationing would disappear and that we should return to an era of plenty. I received an endless number of petitions asking for an increase in the rations.

One industrialist from Lombardy, a man who had been a Minister, came and suggested to me an immediate increase in the bread ration of 500 grammes. 'But I have not got ten million quintals of grain to last till the next harvest.' 'No people has ever died of hunger,' replied the ex-minister, 'and certainly things will right themselves gradually.'

Such irresponsibility was one of the numerous signs of the complete lack of understanding of the situation.

⁕   ⁕   ⁕

Many of the intellectuals simply ignored the war; all

[1] English text by permission of the author and the editor of the *Contemporary Review*.

they were interested in was to destroy every vestige of
Fascism. Very few troubled to remember that in twenty
years it had penetrated into every branch of national life.
There was hardly an organization which was not completely dominated by the Party. Precipitate action would
have resulted in an entire paralysis of the life of the
country because it was impossible to find new staffs in
the course of a few days.

A certain number of these intellectuals acted in good
faith, being really inspired by the desire to provide the
country with free institutions, but others were animated
by anger at the wrongs they had suffered. And however
bitter the truth is, it must be added that there were many
who merely wanted the posts for themselves and these
were naturally the most active.

꙳   ꙳   ꙳

I must say something about the attitude of the civil
servants. They had watched with amazement the instan-
taneous collapse of the régime but were not convinced that
the new government would last. So they did not hesitate
to whittle down the orders they received and to carry on
a secret passive resistance. The machine did not stop but
it worked very slowly.

꙳   ꙳   ꙳

But it was obvious after the first moment of stupefaction
that the most active members of the Party would try to
carry on, relying entirely on the support of the Germans—
the only hope of salvation that remained to them. A
certain number of the most dangerous were arrested to
be dealt with by legal methods, but the number was so
great that it was physically impossible to arrest them all.
Quietly but persistently, the residue preached that Fascism

had arisen from the need to combat Communism and that if it disappeared completely there would be a bolshevist dictatorship. They nicknamed my Government 'Kerensky' and prophesied that an Italian Lenin would arise.

This conviction was explained to me at length during a conversation which I had with Federzoni and Grandi a few days after I became Head of the Government. I told them that whatever was the eventual outcome, it would certainly be better than Fascism, which had corrupted the soul of the nation and finally led the country to its present desperate straits.

CHAPTER VII

The New Government and the German Reaction

I WENT at an early hour on 26 July to the Viminale Palace which had been the seat of the last democratic governments. As I arrived there broke out a lively exchange of fire between the guard there and a detachment of Militia anti-aircraft gunners who were in charge of some machine-guns on the roof of a house opposite. The firing lasted intermittently for about an hour: finally it came to an end when a senior officer intervened at my orders.

I was told that the German Ambassador, von Mackensen, wanted to see me. He was a man with a very disagreeable expression, he looked menacing even when he wanted to be amiable. He at once presented me with a written protest against the attack by the crowd on the German Consulate in Turin. I replied that as I had only just assumed control of the new Government I had not seen any of my officials so I did not know what had occurred but would make inquiries.

But this was only a preamble. Von Mackensen then expressed his anger at what had happened, observing that the fall of Mussolini and of Fascism had amazed German public opinion, had undermined faith in their Italian ally, and had infuriated the Führer who was an old and devoted friend of the Duce.

I replied with complete calm that it was not the fault of the present Government if the Führer and the German people had not been informed for some time of the real state of public opinion in Italy. For more than a year the people had shown clearly their hatred of Fascism and war.

Anyone who did not shut himself up in an ivory tower or was not blind or deaf must have known the state of their feelings. I remarked that Fascism had fallen with hardly any reaction which proved that it did not represent any living forces in the nation. As I had to go to the King to be sworn in, the conversation then ended.

In the afternoon the new ministers came to see me, except the Minister for Foreign Affairs, who was in Turkey.[1] After a few words of welcome I told them that on Tuesday morning they would have to be sworn in and that the first meeting of the Cabinet would be at 6 p.m. that day.

I was convinced that the German Government would have to be told that Italy must make peace. This was the step that Mussolini had not dared to take at Feltre on 19 July and though it was not likely that the Germans would agree, I still wished to tell them that we could not continue the war.

On 27 July, on orders from the King, I telegraphed to Hitler notifying him of the change of Government and suggesting a meeting in Italy to examine the situation, saying that the King would be present. I laid down that the meeting should be in Italy because I was sure that if I went to Germany I should never return.

But even before I received a reply to my proposal there was news from the frontier which put an end to all doubts. Across all the passes (Tarvisio, Brenner, Resia, Dobbiaco, Mont Cenis, Ventimiglia) there had been a continuous stream of German forces pouring down into Italy ever

[1] Signor Guariglia, a career diplomatist. (*Translator.*)

since 26 July. In all, at least eight divisions and a brigade had spread themselves successively over Liguria, Friuli, Giulia, Romagna, and Tuscany. Germany had thrown off her mask and had immediately taken the necessary measures to ensure her possession of the Lombard plain. So when I received Hitler's reply sent through von Ribbentrop, saying that as he had had a discussion with Mussolini on 19 July, he considered that another meeting would be useless, I had already made up my mind.

I appreciated the necessity of temporizing with the Germans as far as possible and at the same time of doing everything in my power to get into touch with the British and Americans.

I knew that this decision would give rise to grave doubts as to my loyalty as Head of the Government and to the loyalty of the country which I represented. Unfortunately that accusation had been levelled at Italy for her declaration of neutrality in 1914 and still more so when she intervened on the side of the Allies in 1915. However, it was clear that a continuation of the war would bring complete ruin on my country. Believing in the truth of the maxim *Salus patriae suprema lex*, I did not hesitate to assume this tremendous responsibility.

I was also sure that if I could get into touch with the Allies I could obtain better terms than the 'unconditional surrender' on which the English continued to insist.

⌁   ⌁   ⌁

On the following day the first meeting of the Cabinet was held; this was entirely taken up with a review of the internal situation. The people, very rightly, were demanding rapid and drastic action against Fascism and the immediate punishment of the guilty. With regard to the first, the question was immensely complicated. As I have already pointed out, in twenty years Fascism had penetrated and dominated every section of our national life, including all state and semi-state organizations of every kind, while all the important posts in the provinces and in the communes were held by Fascists. To change all this at a single blow was not only physically impossible, but if it had been attempted would have entirely paralysed the country. Therefore it was essential to begin first of all with the chief organs at the centre and work out to the periphery.

It was decided first of all to announce the dissolution of the Fascist Party, the Fascist Grand Council, the Supreme Tribunal for the Defence of the State, and the Chamber of Fasces and Corporations. As for the Youth Movement, that mammoth organization which had cost one milliard, eight hundred million lire a year, it was decided to break it up and to entrust the sections to different Ministers so that its valuable properties should not be dispersed. On the other hand it was convenient to allow the so-called 'After-Work Organization' to continue as it provided many benefits and amusements for the workers; when remodelled by the appointment of a Commissioner and by the gradual elimination of Fascist influences, it could carry on its very useful welfare work.

The post of 'Federal Secretary' was abolished, for the only business of these Fascist officials was to supervise the work of the prefects and to run the communes through their own political secretaries. This was a typical example of Fascist organization for it enabled the central Government to thrust its tentacles into even the smallest local groups. With very rare exceptions these 'Federal Secretaries' were the real despots of the provinces and were generally known as *rases*.[1]

[1] Italian slang for a political 'boss'. (*Translator*.)

In subsequent meetings of the Cabinet we went on with our task of righting the wrongs that Fascism had done to all those who in any way opposed the Party. It is impossible for me to give a complete account of all that we did, depending as I am entirely on my memory, but I shall try to sum up what we achieved and to describe all the obstacles that we had to overcome.

It is well known that every government depends on the prefects of the various provinces for the carrying out of its orders and instructions.[1] The situation in this respect was both grave and dangerous. More than half the prefects were creatures of the Fascist régime, chosen from among ex-Federal Secretaries or leading supporters who obeyed the Party blindly and were not as a rule trained to do anything else.

It was decided to supersede them as rapidly as possible and to appoint career prefects who were employed in various posts at the Ministry of the Interior and to recall others who had recently retired. The Minister of the Interior was told to report at a subsequent meeting on the steps he had taken. To the general surprise it was discovered when the list was produced that only eight prefects had been dismissed, and these were unknown rascals who had been in charge of the least important provinces. The Cabinet was very angry and the Minister was invited to present a further list of dismissals which was not to omit one prefect of Fascist origin. I saw the Minister privately after the Cabinet to spur him on to action.

But information very soon reached me that the person who was behind the vacillating Minister was the Minister of the Royal Household, who had intervened personally. I sent for the Duke Acquarone and reminded him that in

---

[1] i.e. in countries where the administration is based on the Code Napoléon; under normal conditions the prefects are trained civil servants. (*Translator.*)

former days Crispi had asked for the resignation of the
Minister of the Royal Household because he had inter-
fered with political affairs. There was no doubt that the
present Minister was doing the same thing. As a matter
of fact when I decided to appoint Senator Ricci Minister
of the Interior, the King made no objection.

Ricci, who had been trained as a Prefect himself, was
competent and forceful and acted quickly and energetically; he removed more than fifty prefects. As a result
the position in the provinces improved, but a month
elapsed before all the new prefects had taken up their
appointments and were sufficiently conversant with the
state of affairs to act with confidence.

My endeavours to remove Fascist diplomatists were
limited by the action of the King. I suggested to him the
dismissal of all ambassadors who were leading Fascists, but
the King sent me a memorandum in which he laid down
that only those who had actually committed crimes should
be retired as it was not the moment to punish representatives of the former régime. This memorandum was left in
the safe at the Viminale, where it was later found by the
Fascists and is referred to by Mussolini in his book, *The
Story of a Year*.

But the general public did not understand why so many
Fascists continued to occupy their former posts and began
to grumble against the Government.

৽   ৽   ৽

Another urgent matter was the question of the press and
of propaganda which came under the Minister of Popular
Culture. A former member of the Ministry of Foreign
Affairs had been chosen for this post; he was trustworthy
and intelligent but new to the work and it was soon
obvious that he was not competent to control so turbulent

an organization. He was succeeded by the former ambassador Galli who I knew was capable of dealing with the many intrigues which were going on.

ᖰ⸱   ᖰ⸱   ᖰ⸱

The future of the various kinds of Fascist Militia was a peculiarly thorny problem. During the first years of Fascism it consisted of volunteers, but later, with the increase in the number of battalions, voluntary enlistment did not produce enough men, and recourse was had to conscription. All members of the Party (and everyone who worked for his living had to belong to the Party) were liable to military service and were called up either for the armed forces or the Militia. We found that while the country was at war it was not possible to disband all the battalions of the Militia without inflicting a grave injustice on the army, and a temporary solution had to be sought. The Militia battalions were incorporated into the army, deprived of all their Fascist badges, and all officers who were ardent Fascists were removed. The headquarters staff was reorganized, an energetic and loyal general being appointed in command. Similar steps were taken with the Frontier, Forestry, the Anti-Aircraft, the Port, the Roads, and other Militia formations. Special care was devoted to the 'Mussolini Battalions' which consisted of young and fanatical volunteers, whom the Germans had provided with tanks to constitute an armoured division. General Calvi de Bergolo[1] was given command of this division and showed much energy in getting rid of the undesirable elements.

It had always been Mussolini's dream to create his own army, devoted to himself. The Fascist leaders, especially Bottai, went so far as to assert that all the infantry should

[1] The King's son-in-law. (*Translator.*)

be Fascist 'Legionaries'. The plan, however, was never officially sponsored by the Duce and was only partially put into effect.

∾·   ∾·   ∾·

While these general measures were being put into force and important posts were being filled by men of undoubted competence and honesty, we proceeded to arrest the most dangerous elements, Fascists who were notorious for their devotion to the régime or for their criminal antecedents: the President of the Special Tribunal for the Defence of the State, Tringali,[1] Buffarini Guidi,[2] Bottai, Teruzzi,[3] Marshal Cavallero (because of his close relations with Farinacci), and Muti,[4] who in trying to resist arrest was shot by the Carabinieri. Farinacci managed to escape to Munich and Ciano disappeared.

∾·   ∾·   ∾·

Three other measures were carried out by the Government at this time. A special Commission of Judges under the President of the Court of Cassation, was set up to examine all the fortunes which had been made under Fascism and after proper inquiry to sequestrate for the benefit of the State all money which had been obtained

[1] Casanuovo Tringali, member of the Special Tribunal for the Defence of the State, 1928; President, 1932; Minister of Justice in the Neo-Fascist Republic, 1943; died of apoplexy 1 November 1943. (*Translator.*)

[2] Guido Guidi Buffarini, personal friend of Mussolini; Under-Secretary for Internal Affairs, 1942–3; Minister for Internal Affairs Neo-Fascist Republic, 1943; captured by the Patriots and executed 7 July 1945. (*Translator.*)

[3] Attilio Teruzzi, commanded a division in Abyssinia, 1936; Minister for Italian East Africa, 1938–43; after the liberation sentenced to thirty years' imprisonment as a collaborator. (*Translator.*)

[4] Ettore Muti, fought in First World War at the age of fourteen; fought in Abyssinia and Spain; Secretary Fascist Party, 1939–40; pilot in the Air Force; arrested during the 'purge' and shot trying to escape, 24 August 1943.

illegally. This was very popular with the public and the denunciations ran into thousands. Subsequently the 'Fascist Republic' declared on the wireless that I had not discovered a new method of procedure because the law bore the stamp of Fascism. It was not the law but the fortunes which certainly bore the stamp of Fascism!

The second measure related to the Jews. It was not possible at that moment to abrogate publicly all the racial laws without coming into violent conflict with the Germans, or, to be more accurate, with Hitler. He had not only inspired this legislation, he had actually forced it on Mussolini, who only a few months earlier had declared in the Senate that there was no Jewish problem in Italy. I sent for representative Jews and told them that, though it was not possible at the moment to revoke the laws, they would not be carried out.

The third measure was the release of all those who had been sent to prison or *confino*[1] for their political opinions. It was necessary to ascertain that the sentence was solely for political reasons, and this took a certain amount of time, while the lack of shipping made it very difficult to provide transport for those who were detained on the Islands. The press demanded more rapid action on the part of the Government, but everything possible was being done. So ended this shameful chapter in the Fascist tyranny.

◦   ◦   ◦

There was great anxiety about the state of our finances. Nothing was really known, but it was clear that while there were no new loans to be taken up almost compulsorily by the banks, new notes were being printed,

[1] *Confino* included banishment to the Lipari Islands, house arrest, or an order to reside in a particular locality. It was not confined to political prisoners. (*Translator.*)

especially those of a high value. I begged the Minister of Finance for a comprehensive statement on our monetary position. This statement, first read to the Cabinet and then published in the papers, made the very gravest impression. The public debt was more than six hundred milliards of lire, and one milliard of notes was in circulation. The Minister pointed out that the situation was even worse because of the financial disorder which existed in the many semi-state organizations.

      ◊   ◊   ◊

I will conclude this chapter with a brief account of the action of the Government with regard to Mussolini. As I have already said, he was taken to a Carabinieri barracks in Rome, but this, of course, was only a temporary measure. Mussolini wished to go to his summer residence, Rocca delle Caminate, but the prefect of Bologna, although an ardent Fascist, refused to accept the responsibility; he declared that no guard would be able to prevent the infuriated people from seizing the ex-dictator and dealing out summary justice.

Mussolini's family were taken to Rocca for their own security, although his wife and children were not regarded as sharing responsibility for his actions. He was transferred to the Island of Ponza, but after a few days we had to remove him to La Maddalena because everyone in Rome knew where he was and talked openly of his whereabouts, so it was to be expected that the Germans would rescue him by a *coup de main*. But the same thing happened over La Maddalena, and with infinite precautions for secrecy he was taken to Campo Imperatore.[1] The result was just the same; this too became common knowledge.

[1] A ski-ing centre, only reached by a funicular, in the heart of the Abruzzi mountains. (*Translator.*)

The Germans annoyed me very much. Keitel at once demanded in the name of the Führer to be allowed to see Mussolini. After my categorical refusal he contented himself with writing an open letter which I sent to Mussolini. Then Hitler intervened personally, forwarding an enormous case containing the works of Nietzsche, beautifully bound and with an affectionate inscription. He incessantly inquired about this present until he had received a personal acknowledgement from Mussolini.

CHAPTER VIII

The Armistice

ON 29 July Signor Guariglia, the Ambassador to Turkey, whom I had proposed to the King as Minister of Foreign Affairs, arrived in Rome by air. I had, and have, the greatest confidence in Guariglia; he is a man of great culture with a quick and penetrating brain and a very pleasant personality.

He came to see me at once and told me that he thoroughly understood my point of view. When he was leaving Istamboul he had spoken very frankly to the Turkish Minister of Foreign Affairs and had begged him to inform the Allied representatives in Turkey that although he (Guariglia) was not empowered to make any communication to their Governments, he could assure them of his conviction that Italy was on the point of changing her policy. I explained the situation to him, and he entirely agreed with me that to keep the proposed negotiations secret it was essential that as few people as possible should know about them. Such a delicate matter could not even be discussed in the Cabinet. I told the Minister of the protests I had made to Berlin through our Military Attaché and to Marshal Kesselring, Commanding German forces in Italy, over the dispatch of German troops to Italy, protests to which I had received no reply.

I also told him that I had asked the Chief of the General Staff if we had sufficient troops to oppose the entry of the Germans; General Ambrosio had replied that it was quite impossible to take any action in view of the small number of men at our disposal, while their dispersal made a rapid concentration impossible.

F

Guariglia then said that he had immediately got into touch with the British Minister to the Holy See[1] as well as the American Chargé d'Affaires, to find out if it was possible to establish communication between their Governments and that of Italy. The British Minister informed us that unfortunately his secret code was very old and almost certainly known to the Germans and that he could not advise us to use it for a secret communication to his Government. The American Chargé d'Affaires replied that he had not got a secret code. Mr. Osborne promised to ask his Government for a new code which would be absolutely safe, but at the moment it was impossible for us to use this means of establishing communication.

On 1 August I received a telegram from Hitler in which he proposed a conference at Tarvisio on 6 August in order to examine the situation, Germany to be represented by von Ribbentrop and Marshal Keitel. I let Guariglia know immediately, and, in order not to arouse suspicions in the minds of the Germans, we decided to agree. It was equally important not to arouse suspicions in the minds of the British and Americans, and we decided to take the following steps:

1. To send an official of the Foreign Office to Lisbon in order to explain Italian policy to the Allied Powers. This official was to make it clear that we were agreeing to the conference at Tarvisio in order to lull the suspicions of the Germans, which were increasing every day, and in order to avoid their taking more drastic measures against us than those from which we were suffering at the moment. This communication was to be forwarded to the Governments in London and Washington on 4 August.

2. To send an official of the Foreign Office to Tangier

[1] Now Sir D'Arcy Osborne. (*Translator.*)

to make a similar communication to the British
Minister in that town.

3. To avail ourselves of a special train, which was leaving
   for Lisbon on 12 August with some Foreign Office
   officials, to send a military mission to negotiate an
   armistice.

General Ambrosio proposed that General Castellano
should be sent, accompanied by Dr. Montanari of the
Foreign Office who spoke perfect English. I explained to
General Ambrosio that General Castellano, besides discussing the terms of the armistice, must describe the
tragedy of our position—the whole of Italy occupied by
the Germans, and the absolute necessity of immediate help
to enable us to face the inevitable and furious German
reaction.

It will be seen from this that I as Head of the Government and Guariglia as Minister of Foreign Affairs did not
neglect anything or lose any time in trying to explain our
policy to the Allies.

The Conference took place at Tarvisio on 6 August in
an atmosphere of doubt and suspicion; it did not reach
any decisions. My insistence, supported by General
Ambrosio, that we should be allowed to bring home the
Italian divisions in Russia and the Balkans in view of the
imminent threat to the whole of Europe, was rejected.

The Allied Governments showed that they understood
and accepted Guariglia's explanation of our action. Their
press and their wireless hardly mentioned the Conference
and did not make any ill-advised comments. This represented our only positive success.[1]

[1] Guariglia informed the Cabinet what had been discussed; I decided on

When all the questions relating to the request for an armistice had been settled, I sent for General Ambrosio to decide on the measures to be taken to safeguard La Spezia, our chief naval base, from a German *coup de main*: to ensure that Rome would be able to offer a certain amount of resistance we decided to concentrate in the neighbourhood five complete divisions and, in addition, the elements of two other divisions to be entrusted to an energetic commander. General Carboni, who was chosen for this post on the advice of General Ambrosio, was Chief of the Army Staff.

In order to understand fully the subsequent defence of Rome I think it is essential to explain exactly what steps were taken. In agreement with the Minister of Foreign Affairs Rome was once again declared an 'open city'. This had been done by Mussolini, but he subsequently ignored his own declaration. The Germans, although they were annoyed, did not raise any serious objections; as a matter of fact, however, it remained a unilateral declaration, never having been accepted by the British and Americans. Nevertheless, we complied with all the necessary formalities; all the military headquarters were removed and were established outside the limits of the 'open city', the perimeter of the protected zone being about seventeen miles. The Swiss Minister in Rome was asked to assume control of all the measures which we announced.

Our forces took up positions on the perimeter, and therefore their lines were very thin; although they could have offered some resistance they could not beat off an armoured

this course as I knew how anxious my fellow ministers were for news. I followed Guariglia's long statement with a description of our military situation and that of the German troops in Italy. But I did not say anything about my plans, as it was essential for secrecy that these should be known to as few people as possible. Naturally I did not mention the steps for obtaining an armistice.

column. We had not enough troops to provide a more adequate line of defence.

I and the General also drew up instructions which were to be sent to all commanding officers in Italy and in other theatres of war as to their line of conduct in the event of an armistice. Wherever possible these orders were to be carried by officers who were to arrive at the crucial moment. General Ambrosio told me that, as such a contingency had been in his mind for some time, the instructions were almost ready and it was only necessary to give them the final touches.

∾   ∾   ∾

Two other events at this time made me more anxious than ever to settle things as quickly as possible.

At the suggestion of the Germans a conference was held at Bologna, attended by Italian and German officers, to discuss questions relating to the positions held by German and Italian troops. This meeting also was held in an atmosphere of mutual distrust and was dominated to a certain extent by lightly veiled German threats. No decisions were arrived at.

On 17 August the Italo-German forces, in the face of superior numbers and equipment, were forced to abandon Sicily.

∾   ∾   ∾

General Castellano reached Rome on 28 August, bringing with him the terms of the armistice.[1] I spent a day

[1] General Castellano had reached Lisbon on 17 August; on 19 August he had seen General Bedell Smith, Chief of the Allied Staff in the Mediterranean, Brigadier Strong, Chief of Allied Intelligence, Sir Ronald Campbell, British Ambassador, and Mr. Kennan, American Chargé d'Affaires. He had been handed the terms of the armistice '. . . to be accepted or rejected . . .'. The delay in his return was caused by the necessity to wait for

examining them most carefully as they seemed to me to be very harsh and in some instances impossible to carry out. I then went to see the King to explain the situation to him. On 30 August I received General Ambrosio, General Castellano, and the Minister of Foreign Affairs in my office and instructed Castellano to proceed to Sicily the following day as he had arranged with the Allied High Command. He was to explain that Italy was not in a position to carry out the armistice terms as her armed forces were so much weaker than those of the Germans and would quickly be wiped out; the Government would conclude an armistice when the Allies had landed at least fifteen divisions in a suitable locality.

General Castellano saw General Bedell Smith, Chief of Staff to General Eisenhower, on 31 August. He stated that the terms communicated in Lisbon could not be altered, that the Italian Government could only accept or reject them. He added that the Allies would first of all disembark three or four divisions on the mainland to draw off the German forces, and then a few days later the fifteen divisions would be landed in a different place. Six hours before the principal landing General Eisenhower would announce over the wireless the acceptance of our request for an armistice, and immediately afterwards we were to make a similar announcement on the wireless.

General Castellano tried to find out at least where the principal landing would take place so that we might make proper dispositions, but General Bedell Smith refused to give the slightest indication. He said in addition that if the terms were not accepted very much heavier conditions would be imposed on Italy, that all the cities, including

the return of the special train; he had to spend the time in hiding for fear that he or, even worse, the armistice terms, might be discovered and seized by the Germans. (*Translator.*)

Rome, would be razed to the ground and all our industries destroyed. In later confidential discussions, when it was known that the Allies would not land north of Rome as we wished them to do, General Castellano and General Bedell Smith worked out a plan for the defence of the city. It was agreed that on the night of the armistice an airborne division should be landed on the outskirts, while an armoured division should disembark at the mouth of the Tiber.

On 1 September, after General Castellano's return from Sicily, I held another meeting of Guariglia, Ambrosio, and Castellano: they were all in favour of accepting the terms proposed. I went immediately to see the King to receive his orders and then informed Ambrosio that the armistice was to be accepted.

Castellano returned to Sicily on 2 September, and on 3 September the armistice was signed. All the relevant documents were brought to Rome on 5 September by Major Marchesi who had accompanied General Castellano to Sicily. It was laid down that the date of the armistice would be between 10 and 15 September, and according to an official communication from General Bedell Smith it would probably be 12 September. Among the documents were the orders for the airborne division, which needed co-operation on our part, operations which would take not less than seven days. General Ambrosio in submitting the documents therefore confirmed that we could regard 12 September as the official date.

About 2 a.m. on 8 September General Carboni, the American General Taylor, and another American officer arrived at my house. General Taylor had come to arrange with our High Command for the landing of the airborne division, but as the Chief of the General Staff was absent from Rome and would only return at 10 a.m. the following

day, General Carboni on his own initiative had brought
the American officers to my house. General Taylor, a fine
soldier (he had been among the cadets I had inspected at
West Point in 1921), told me that, contrary to what had
been said, the armistice was imminent and would perhaps
be declared that very day, 8 September.

I said that for reasons of safety the airborne division
could only begin its landing on the night of 9 September
and that as he had stated it would take four or five days
to land the whole division, this operation could not coincide with the principal landing if this took place on
8 September. General Carboni then said that he would
need some days to complete the issue of ammunition and
petrol to his army corps.

In view of these facts I drafted a telegram to General
Eisenhower in which, after referring to the desire of the
Italian Government to collaborate and for an opportunity
to prove its loyalty to the Allied cause, I insisted that the
armistice should be postponed till 12 September as had
originally been laid down, in the interest of military operations. During the morning of 8 September the Chief of the
General Staff returned and prepared a communication to
the Allies asking them to modify some of the operations
and to postpone the armistice at least to 12 September.
This note, which I approved, was given to General Rossi,
the Deputy Chief of the General Staff, who, after having
obtained the consent of the Allies, left at once by air for
Allied Headquarters.

೧   ೧   ೧

Here I should explain that General Castellano, on his
return from Lisbon, brought with him a radio set which he
had been given by the Allied High Command, with an
American secret code. In this way we were able after

29 August to be in constant touch with the Allied High Command in Algiers.

At 5.30 p.m. on 8 September a telegram in code signed by General Eisenhower arrived in which the Italian Government was required to declare the armistice at 8 p.m. If this was not done, General Eisenhower declared that the armistice signed on 3 September would no longer be valid, and that the negotiations conducted up to that time by the Italian Government with the Allied High Command would be broadcast from Algiers and London.

I was astounded to receive this telegram. I only discovered very much later that the Allied High Command, being very fully informed of the situation in Italy, was afraid that my Government would be overthrown by the Germans and that therefore the armistice would not take effect. The Allied High Command wished to prevent delay and to expedite matters.

It was a decision which entirely upset our plans and brought us to the brink of ruin. General Eisenhower admitted this later when on the evening of 8 September he heard from General Rossi the reasons why we insisted that the armistice should be postponed till 12 September. He said frankly, 'I am inclined to believe that I have made a mistake, but all that matters now is to collaborate to the best of our ability in our common interest.' General Eisenhower showed from that moment such an understanding of our needs, such compassion for the fate of our unfortunate country, as to compensate for the troubles and the sufferings which this hurried decision caused us.

I went immediately to the King, accompanied by the Minister to the Royal Household, the Ministers of Foreign Affairs, of the Army, the Navy, and the Air Force, the Chief of the General Staff, the Deputy Chief of the Army

General Staff (the Chief was absent on duty), General Carboni, and Major Marchesi. It was 6.15 p.m.

General Ambrosio explained the situation, saying that the anticipation of the armistice found our troops in the act of taking up new positions. The Minister of the Army and General Carboni did not believe that the British and Americans would carry out their undertakings and, as the German reaction might be violent, they were in favour of rejecting the armistice. Major Marchesi pointed out the serious harm it would do us to repudiate the conditions signed on 3 September, even if the Allies did not entirely fulfil their promises. The Minister of Foreign Affairs declared that now more than ever it was essential to 'go on to the end'. I then spoke and explained that there were only two possible courses—either His Majesty must publicly repudiate what I had done, declaring that I had acted without his knowledge and dismiss me as Head of the Government, or else we must accept the conditions imposed by the British and Americans whatever the consequences might be. The King expressed the view that a change of policy was now out of the question and that we must acquiesce in the armistice terms.

Meanwhile our information service warned us that the B.B.C. had broadcast a message which said that Italy had asked for an armistice and shortly afterwards announced that General Eisenhower had declared that the Allied Governments had agreed to the request of the Italian Government. It was not possible to delay for a moment. The meeting broke up, and I went at once to the Rome broadcasting station and made the following announcement:

Recognizing the impossibility of continuing the war in face of the overwhelming strength of the enemy, and in order to save the nation from further and even greater disasters, the

Italian Government has asked General Eisenhower, Commander-in-Chief of the Allied Forces, for an armistice.

This request has been acceded to.

In consequence all hostilities by the Italian armed forces against the British and American forces must now cease. They will, however, repel attacks from whatever quarter they may come.

The communiqué was recorded and repeated at frequent intervals.

                                       ◇   ◇   ◇

At the same time the Minister of Foreign Affairs arranged to inform Berlin, Budapest, Bucharest, and Sofia by telegram.

CHAPTER IX

From Rome to Brindisi

As it seemed desirable to give a consecutive account of so important a matter as our relations with the Allies, I have omitted other events which were happening concurrently as they were not relevant to my main thesis. So I must now take up again the story of the work of the Government, of the action of the political parties, and, finally, of our relations with the Germans.

The Government continued its policy of the elimination of Fascism energetically at the centre and at a slower pace in the provinces, owing to the difficulties created by the appointment of the new prefects.

Buozzi and Roveda, a socialist and a communist, were nominated as heads of the workers' syndicates, and their intervention in the cities in the north served to restrain the hotheads. The Committee of Judges, which was to deal with the cases of graft and peculation, had already begun its work, and it was hoped that after proper consideration it would arrive at concrete results. Men chosen with great care were appointed as directors of the semi-state organizations, the banks, and other large concerns.

The Government received information, which immediately spread like wildfire, that a general strike was being organized as a protest against the continuation of the war. This was to take place on 1 September. When I consulted the heads of the various political parties they unanimously declared that they had not organized the strike, and they immediately said that they would publish a manifesto urging the workers to pay no attention to propaganda which came from the enemies of the country. The manifesto appeared in the press on 30 and 31 August, and the strike did not take place.

It was quite clear who was planning this blow to the maintenance of order; the Nazis wanted to prove that at this critical moment the Italian Government could not govern; they wanted to bring about its downfall and then to organize the nomination of a new government entirely subservient to Germany, or else the appointment of a government composed of Fascist and German elements.

As the plan did not succeed, the Germans decided that it would be easier and more profitable to strike at the existing Government by the elimination of its Head. On the morning of 2 September, as soon as I arrived at my office, the Chief of our Information Service came to assure me that the S.S. in Rome were going to assassinate me. This news was shortly afterwards confirmed by the General Commanding the Carabinieri and by the Chief of Police, H. E. Sensi. They told me that the attack was to be carried out when I was leaving or entering my house. Mussolini had favoured the establishment in Rome of this German police force under a certain Dolman. Sensi told me he had not been able to find out the exact number of its agents, but they certainly amounted to over 6,000. They had occupied hotels and private premises to which no one was admitted, but he had been able to plant some reliable informers among them.

I thought the only solution was to tell the German authorities that I knew what was being planned. I therefore sent Guariglia to the German Embassy to denounce the conspiracy and to tell the German Ambassador that I should leave the Viminale Palace at twelve noon punctually and the route I should follow in returning to my house. So if an attack was made on me all the world would know that the Germans were responsible.

This had the desired effect; no attack was made. The next day a telegram arrived from von Ribbentrop in which he declared that the whole thing was purely imaginary as the foreign policy of Germany was directed only by Hitler. He asked for the names of the informers. An attempt at assassination was therefore one of the activities which came under the heading of 'foreign policy'.

       ✧   ✧   ✧

As I had foreseen, von Mackensen did not long remain Ambassador in Italy and was recalled to Germany. He was succeeded by Rahn who had been Gauleiter in Bohemia where he had become famous for his ruthless oppression. He came to see me and engaged me in a long discussion. He began by saying that the fall of Mussolini and the destruction of the Fascist Party had angered the Führer as they menaced the existence of National Socialism which he regarded as the direct outcome of Fascism. Rahn also said that in Germany there was now the greatest distrust of Italy and of the Italian Government of which I was Head. The only way to lessen this distrust was by taking immediately three important and decisive steps. Accordingly he suggested that I should: (1) suspend all action against former members of the Fascist Party; (2) hand over the command of all the Italian armed forces to Marshal Rommel, who was in command of the German troops in Italy; (3) not offer any opposition to the Marshal's plans. He did not wish to turn all Italy into a battlefield, but to concentrate his forces on a line between La Spezia and Rimini, there to give battle to the invader.

Naturally my answer was a complete refusal. I told him that the Government by its elimination of Fascism was only carrying out the clearly expressed wish of the

Italian people, who were determined to have nothing more to do with that corrupt tyranny. As for Rommel's strategic plan, I observed that this was entirely opposed to the ideas so many times expressed by Marshal Kesselring (up to that moment commanding German troops in Italy) who wanted to defend the peninsula step by step, and that—anyhow—we would never agree to abandoning two-thirds of our territory without fighting. Rahn asked me to think over the facts he had stated, declaring that he would come and see me again for further discussions. But events did not allow him to pay me this unwelcome visit.

There was another episode at this time to which I must refer in passing.

One morning (I do not remember the exact date) the sensational news spread through Rome that Hitler had been killed. There were always a great many German troops on leave in Rome and almost all of them began noisy and joyful demonstrations, shouting, kissing each other, and fraternizing gaily with our men. It was undoubtedly a quite spontaneous demonstration and only suppressed by tanks with machine-guns which very soon were driving through the streets in every direction.

I have already explained that I had given orders to the Chief of the General Staff to prepare suitable instructions for the various commands on the action to be taken if we succeeded in obtaining an armistice. These instructions were not to be sent out in advance to prevent their falling into the hands of the Germans. But on the morning of 3 September it seemed to me inadvisable to wait any

longer and I held a meeting in my office of the Ministers
of Foreign Affairs, the Army, Navy, and Air Force; after
explaining the situation I gave orders to proceed at once
with the communication of these instructions so that all the
commanding officers might know what action to take. The
Chief of Staff said that some days previously he had on his
own responsibility sent the orders secretly to the Generals
Commanding in Sardinia and Corsica, and that he would
send similarly to the Headquarters of the Army Group on
the Eastern Front. I once again discussed with General
Ambrosio the defence of Rome, because I wanted to be
certain that it was properly organized, and he assured me
that General Carboni had the matter well in hand. He
had instructed Carboni that if unforeseen circumstances
obliged the Government and the military chiefs to quit the
city he was to assume the command of the divisions outside as well as inside the city and to conduct the defence.
This set my mind at rest and I was sure that everything
possible had been done to prepare for the very grave situation in which we should undoubtedly find ourselves.[1]

❧   ❧   ❧

On the evening of 8 September, after I had read my
proclamation of the armistice over the wireless, I went
straight to the Ministry of War. I was convinced that in
order to forestall a probable attack by the S.S. it would
be advisable to take up my quarters there together with
the royal family and the Chief of the General Staff. The
Minister of War had given orders for a strong detachment of troops to be on duty inside and outside the build-
ing to protect it from a possible German attack. From it
I could also communicate by telephone or wireless with

[1] For his own account of his actions see General Carboni's book,
L'Armistizio e la Defesa di Roma, Verità e Menzogne. (*Translator.*)

everyone. After eating some food I went to lie down in a room which had been prepared for me, for I was completely worn out by the emotions of the day. At 4 a.m. I was awakened because there was serious news, and in another room I found the Minister of War, the Chief of the General Staff, and the Chief of the Army Staff, General Roatta. Roatta described to me in the gloomiest terms the situation of our troops who were being violently attacked by armoured detachments and German parachute contingents; they were already engaged in an indecisive action at the Porta S. Paolo.[1] He was of opinion that, given the strength of the attack, the defence could not last very much longer, and therefore to avoid the capture of the King, the royal family, and the Government it was necessary that we should leave immediately by the one route which was still open, the Via Tiburtina.[2]

General Roatta added that to prevent grave damage to the city, and the troops being defeated in scattered encounters, he had given orders to General Carboni to concentrate his forces and to fall back on Tivoli, where the nature of the ground would allow of a much more efficacious defence. General Ambrosio made no comment on Roatta's statement.

It was a momentous decision which I had to take and I had to take it in the utmost haste. I had to consider all the factors. For me one question was of capital importance and overmastered all the others—that was the necessity to maintain at all costs a close and continuous contact with the Allies, so that the armistice, signed by my orders by General Castellano, might continue in operation. As long as it did so Italy would be treated not as an enemy nation, but as a nation which had solemnly declared her

[1] The gate by the Protestant Cemetery. (*Translator.*)
[2] By the Porta S. Lorenzo. (*Translator.*)

intention to make common cause with the British and
Americans. If the Government remained in Rome its
capture would be inevitable and the Germans would
rapidly substitute a Fascist Government who would repudiate the armistice. This disaster must be avoided at
all costs, for it would mean the complete ruin of Italy.

That my belief was correct was shown later by events
in Hungary. In that country Admiral Horthy, having
proclaimed an armistice in the morning, was immediately
arrested by the Germans and obliged to cancel his former
announcement and to declare that Hungary would continue the war. Everyone knows the terrible consequences
of that declaration for his unfortunate country.

There was another vital question—the fate of Rome.
Everything possible for the defence of the capital had
been done, but the situation described by General Roatta
did not admit of any delay. It was essential to take an
immediate decision so as to avoid the struggle spreading
to the centre of the city with the inevitable result of fire
and ruin.

All these considerations brought me to one conclusion—
it was to leave at all costs and try to reach the south so as
to remain in touch with the Allies.

But this decision, although it was logical and indisputable, was so repugnant to my feelings as a soldier that it
caused me the greatest suffering. How would my desert-
ing the scene of the fighting be regarded? Would the
people understand the need for my departure or would
they attribute it to the most despicable motives? But this
internal struggle did not last long. My record as a soldier
would show that my action was not the result of unworthy
motives. Every personal consideration must be disre-
garded and the supreme interest of my country must be
paramount.

I said that I approved of the orders given by General Roatta and that I had decided to leave Rome by the Via Tiburtina.

In General Ambrosio's presence I told General Sorice[1] immediately to inform all the ministers what I had decided and named Pescara as the place of meeting. Having given these orders I went down to the apartment where the royal family had spent the night and communicated to the King my determination to leave Rome and try to reach Pescara by the Via Tiburtina. I did not conceal from him that it was impossible to foresee what would happen and that it was quite possible, even probable, that we should all be captured during the journey.

The King did not make any objection, but it must be clearly understood that I alone was responsible for the decision to go to Pescara.

General Ambrosio, who was in charge of the military operations, was present at this conversation; he told me that he still had some orders to give and that he would follow us.

      ❧   ❧   ❧

Perhaps I may be allowed to refer here to one family matter. My son Mario, formerly Consul-General in Tangier, was with me. Without any official post he had helped me very much, both in maintaining the closest touch with the representatives of all the political parties, in receiving large numbers of people, and in discussing with me in the evening all the news he had gathered during the day.

He was with me at the Ministry of War on the night of 8–9 September, and when I decided to leave Rome I ordered him to stay in the city as it was so likely that I

[1] The Minister of War. (*Translator.*)

should not succeed in escaping. Many people know what he did during the months between September and April and I will only say that I am proud of him. On Easter Monday he was arrested through the treachery of a Fascist and was taken to Germany.

ᖷ   ᖷ   ᖷ

We got into five motor-cars and went straight to Tivoli. At least three times we were stopped at control posts, but we were allowed to proceed. Tanks were on the road driving towards Rome, but though we believed that they belonged to the Militia Division, we were not sure because we heard loud shouts in German.

We finally arrived at Crecchio and were the guests of the Duke and Duchess di Bovino, and here the Minister of the Navy joined us. He said that he had wirelessed to Pola and Taranto to send the cruiser *Scipione l'Africano* and two corvettes to Pescara, but he did not know whether these orders had been received and if they had been, whether it would be possible for them to be carried out.

In the afternoon we arrived at the airport of Pescara to be followed by General Ambrosio. I asked him for news of the Minister of War and he said that he had left Sorice in his office very much excited, but he thought that the Minister would join us. At the same time some aeroplanes under the command of Colonel Ranieri arrived, but of the cruiser and the two corvettes there was no sign.

We could not leave in the aeroplanes because the Queen had heart trouble and could not fly. But it was absurd to remain at Pescara for the Germans could reach it without the slightest trouble. Finally, an aeroplane which I had sent on a reconnaissance flight to the north reported that there was a corvette about fifty miles distant, steaming south. We embarked in her at midnight—the royal family,

I, the Ministers of the Navy and the Air Force, the Chief of the General Staff, and my most faithful private secretary, Lieut.-Colonel Valenzano, who had been at my side ever since 1935, sharing with me good and evil fortune. Neither the Minister of War nor any other Cabinet Minister had joined us. In this cockleshell, which was the corvette *Baionetta*, we steamed south without the slightest idea where we could drop anchor.

Arrived at Bari we saw a German reconnaissance plane which circled over us for about twenty minutes at a prudent distance, sending out wireless signals all the time. Perhaps surprised at seeing so many people on the upper deck, she was calling for other planes to come and attack us. Finally we arrived at Brindisi and having sent for Admiral Rubartelli, the Admiral of the Port, we learned that there were at Brindisi a certain number of men of an Italian Coastal Division, and at the moment there was no sign of German or British and American troops.

We disembarked and the sailors gave us a great reception, cheering the King and me.

At last we were ashore, in the city which was the first capital of the new Italy.

~ ~ ~

I have no reports which enable me to express an opinion on the conduct of the various commands at the time of the armistice. Fragmentary and unsubstantiated rumours do not tempt me to give any judgements. It is necessary to remember the difficulties in which these commands found themselves and the aggressiveness and bad faith of many of the German officers. I hope that the inquiry which will certainly be held will take these special circumstances into account. If in some cases weakness was shown, I am sure that there will prove to be many examples of personal initiative, of heroism and self-sacrifice for the sake of the country.

⟨∘⟩   ⟨∘⟩   ⟨∘⟩

The first Allied landing with very small forces took place at the extreme south of Calabria.

The principal landing was made at Salerno.

Neither the airborne division nor the armoured division promised for the defence of Rome appeared on the scene.

PART II

CHAPTER X

First Days at Brindisi

THE first difficulty to be overcome at Brindisi was that of finding accommodation. The royal family was housed in the admiral's quarters, while everyone else, including the Head of the Government, was crowded into some small barracks belonging to the crews of the submarines. A very simple mess was organized to which everybody belonged and where the meals were served at three sittings.

General Ambrosio and General Roatta immediately set about concentrating at Brindisi all the troops engaged in coastal defence, and with these and the naval forces available a defensive line was organized. It was known that the Germans were still at Gioai del Colle, at Matera, and at Bari.

The situation in which I found myself at Brindisi was almost desperate. Only the Ministers for the Navy and for Air were with me, so I immediately sent for H. E. Innocenti, the Prefect of Taranto, who set up an Office of Internal Affairs, of which I shall have more to say later. Making use of the American wireless, which fortunately we had brought from Rome, I was able to get into touch at once with General Eisenhower's headquarters at Algiers and inform him that the King and I had been obliged to leave Rome and that we had taken refuge in Brindisi. I begged him to send a staff officer so that we could be certain of maintaining communications.

General Eisenhower replied immediately, saying that he was sending a commission under the British General Sir Frank Mason-MacFarlane and that meanwhile, with the troops at my disposal, I was to guarantee the security of the ports, of the means of communication, and of the aerodromes, as well as providing the workmen needed to handle the large quantities of supplies which would be landed at the harbours in Puglia.

We had no means of communication with the remainder of Italy. 'Radio Bari' was so weak that it could hardly be heard in Rome, so we decided to issue two proclamations, one signed by the King and the other by me, explaining briefly what had happened and our decision to fight beside the Allies for the liberation of Italy from the German yoke. Copies of these proclamations were dropped with great enthusiasm by our pilots on every Italian city, including Rome.

In order to have some information as to what was happening in Italy and the rest of the world, I ordered General Ambrosio to organize a system for picking up foreign broadcasts, and to issue a news bulletin. The Minister for Air gave valuable help to this undertaking. In this way we heard of the creation of a Republican Fascist Government, of the liberation of Mussolini, which was carried out by German parachute troops dropped in the vicinity of Campo Imperatore, and of the assumption by General Graziani of the command of the Republican armed forces.

I immediately set up my private secretariat; it consisted of only a handful of people, all of whom showed the same spirit of self-sacrifice and capacity for hard work as my inseparable Valenzano. With personnel provided by General Ambrosio we created the first nucleus of a propaganda organization which set about the task of sending out

daily wireless bulletins. Meanwhile two members of the
Foreign Office, Signor Grillo and Signor Stampa, arrived,
having walked from Rome, and I was delighted to hand
over to them the most urgent problems in foreign affairs.
Shortly afterwards Dr. Montanari joined us and with his
perfect knowledge of English he was my most invaluable
and trusted interpreter.

Jung[1] came in an English aeroplane from Palermo; I
knew that he was a financial expert and a most patriotic
man, ready to make any sacrifice for the sake of his
country. Gathering assistants where he could, he succeeded in a short time in creating the essential financial
services which were so warmly praised by the Allies. I
cannot speak too highly of Jung's work; I can only say,
'He deserved well of the State.'

Piccardi, the Minister of Industry and Commerce, made
his way first to Naples and then rejoined the Government
at Brindisi. The post of Minister of War was held for the
moment by the Chief of the General Staff, General
Ambrosio. Signor Mario Fano, a highly trained electrical
engineer, succeeded in making his way from northern
Italy, while among the generals I had with me was Di
Raimondo, the railway expert. So with the help of these
two I set up a Ministry of Communications divided into
sections responsible for railways and posts and telegraphs.

∾   ∾   ∾

On 11 September the following message signed by
Churchill and Roosevelt reached me, having been relayed
from Algiers.

[1] The head of a well-known Sicilian Jewish banking family; he had
served with distinction as an artillery officer in the First World War. He
was Minister of Finance under Mussolini in the early days of Fascism.
(*Translator.*)

Marshal

It has fallen to you in the hour of your country's agony to take the first decisive step to win peace and freedom for the Italian people and to win back for Italy an honourable place in the civilization of Europe. . . . The German terror in Italy will not last long. They will be extirpated from your land and you, by helping in this great surge of liberation, will place yourselves once more among the true and long-proved friends of your country from whom you have been so long estranged. Take every chance you can. Strike hard and strike home. All will come out well. March forward with your American and British friends in the great world movement toward freedom, justice, and peace.[1]

I replied immediately in the following terms:

Everything possible will be done with the same courage and tenacity that we both showed on the fields of battle in Italy and in France during the last world war. I can assure you that the Italian people, under their King, ardently desire at the cost of any sacrifice to obtain liberty and a just peace. They will not fail manfully to do their duty and more than their duty on every occasion. We have faith and we will march with you, our American and English friends.

◇   ◇   ◇

General Mason-MacFarlane, with General Taylor and a staff of about twenty officers, now arrived and took up their headquarters at the International Hotel. I thus got to know General Mason-MacFarlane and worked with him on the most friendly terms for many months. A distinguished Scotsman, the master of many languages, with an accurate mind, he was an expert in European politics and politicians, having held important posts in almost every European country. He was full of sympathy with our unhappy position and did everything in his power

[1] Official text, released by the White House and printed in the *New York Times*, 11 September 1943.

to help us to overcome our difficulties, and supported our requests to the Allied Governments. From being the Chief of the Allied Liaison Commission, he became the Chief of the Allied Control Commission of which I shall have something to say at a later stage.

During our first talk I discussed with him the necessity of my getting into touch with our representatives abroad by means of the British embassies and legations, so that we could send and receive direct communications. The General agreed and so, despite many difficulties and incredible delays, I found out that with very few defections the whole of our diplomatic and consular corps had remained loyal to the King's Government. I also heard that the Germans and Japanese had imprisoned all our representatives in Germany and Japan and in all the countries occupied by these two powers. It makes me very happy to be able to tell my fellow countrymen of the loyal and courageous conduct of practically all our officials abroad, who, notwithstanding the annoyances, the bad treatment, and the threats of reprisals against their families, followed the path of duty and of honour.

General Mason-MacFarlane also agreed to provide transport from Lisbon to Brindisi for our Minister, Signor Prunas, a most devoted and experienced diplomat. I made him Secretary General for Foreign Affairs and with the help of about thirty young officials, who had escaped with considerable danger and difficulty from the Foreign Office in Rome, he set up a Ministry for Foreign Affairs which worked admirably.

·◦·   ·◦·   ·◦·

The Anglo-American political representatives had arrived with General Mason-MacFarlane—Macmillan,[1]

[1] The Rt. Hon. Harold Macmillan, Minister Resident at Allied Headquarters in NW. Africa. (*Translator*.)

Caccia,[1] Murphy,[2] and Riber.[3] With them I discussed what I had achieved: ports, aerodromes, and means of communication had been rendered secure; dockers had been provided at every port capable of handling 5,000 to 15,000 tons of supplies a day; workmen were keeping the roads in order and repairing the railways. But I added that while I knew that the provision of man-power was essential, this alone was not at all satisfactory to the Italians, who were longing to fight to free their country from the Germans.

I pointed out to them that it was certainly true that in the so-called 'Quebec document' it was clearly stated that the conditions of the armistice did not envisage the active assistance of Italy in the war. But, I added, the document also laid down that any modifications of the conditions depended on the amount of support given by the Italian Government and people to the Allies during the remainder of the war. Moreover, the document affirmed that the Allied nations would give the Italian armed forces all possible assistance whenever they attacked the Germans, destroyed German supplies, or obstructed the movement of German troops. I told the Allied representatives that I had consequently telegraphed to General Eisenhower asking for permission for Italian troops to take part in the struggle.

At the same time I submitted to them a problem which was of the greatest importance to me; how could I raise the morale of the Italian people after so many disasters, if I was only in possession of the military terms of the armistice which had been signed by General Castellano on 3 September, while I was still entirely ignorant of the

[1] Major Caccia, a British officer, member of an Anglo-Florentine family. (*Translator.*)

[2] Mr. Robert Murphy, American Minister attached to General Eisenhower's staff. (*Translator.*)

[3] American, assistant to Mr. Murphy. (*Translator.*)

political and administrative clauses? I then made them read the message from Churchill and Roosevelt in which it was clearly stated that now that we had taken our former place by the side of the Allies we must march with our English and American friends against the common enemy. I told them that I had replied giving the very fullest assurances of our determination to march with them, and as this message had been signed by the Heads of the two Governments, it could not be regarded simply as a piece of propaganda but was a precise and binding undertaking to which I had adhered without any reservations. I concluded by saying that if they regarded Mussolini and Fascism as responsible for the war, we who had rebelled against his tyranny and ranged ourselves on their side must be regarded as Allies. This was the only way in which I could galvanize the country and induce it to make fresh sacrifices. The representatives promised to lay my views before their Governments.

As soon as they had left I sent the following telegram to General Eisenhower:

I can assure you that all your requests with regard to the security of the means of communication, ports and aerodromes, and the provision of workmen for the various services, have been entirely complied with. As we fought together in 1917–18 let me remind you that the Italians are not cowards. We asked for the armistice as the war was being carried on against the will of the people, and because we had not the means necessary to free ourselves, but we do not intend to remain idle while our country is being liberated. I therefore beg you as a soldier to allow the Italian troops to be employed beside yours in the struggle against the Germans.

My agonized appeal went straight to the heart of General Eisenhower and he granted my request, as I shall explain later.

There were two essential points on which I insisted from the outset—alliance, and the growing participation of Italian troops in the fighting.

⟡   ⟡   ⟡

Next the financial experts arrived with Lord Rennell of Rodd at their head. He was the son of the British Ambassador in Rome during the First World War, and was therefore well known and popular in Rome. They informed us that they had prepared a special issue of notes, from 1 lira to 1,000 lire which they called 'occupation money', but the exchange would remain at 400 lire to the pound sterling and 100 lire to the dollar. I pointed out that such a high rate of exchange would cause inflation, given the number of notes that their soldiers would have (they were paid ten times as much as ours) and this would upset the market, but Lord Rennell was adamant.

He admitted the necessity for two measures which we proposed—all purchases for the Allies should be made by the Italian Government, and that part of the pay of their officers and other ranks should be kept back to be sent to their families or other recipients whom they might choose. But as a matter of fact inflation began at once. The Allied troops, most of whose rations came out of tins, were prepared to pay any price for fresh food; to give only one example, the price of eggs rose from 5 to 30 lire each.

We returned to this question incessantly both by word of mouth and by means of written memoranda; during the following April we even sent a memorandum to Roosevelt, in which Jung pointed out the necessity in the interests of the Allies themselves, of lowering the rate of exchange. But as long as I was in the Government no notice was taken of this communication.

⟡   ⟡   ⟡

The King wished to intervene personally on the subject of the alliance and the reduction in the rate of exchange and so wrote directly to Roosevelt and the King of England. Roosevelt replied that it was too soon to consider a request for an alliance and that the question of the rate of exchange had been referred to experts. Churchill answered on behalf of the King, declaring that for the moment the exchange must stay where it had been fixed, and that there had never been any question of an alliance.

On about 20 September the political representatives visited me again and handed me the complete text of the Armistice which, they stated, embodied the military, political, and administrative clauses. I took a day to examine the document: there was a change in the conditions signed on 3 September.

We had concluded an armistice consonant with the dignity of Italy, putting an end to hostilities between our troops and the Anglo-American forces. This document was entitled 'The Unconditional Surrender of Italy': after stating that the Allied Governments had accepted the unconditional surrender of Italy, there followed forty-four articles in which were laid down the military, political, and administrative conditions. Many of these could not be carried out, such as the handing over of Allied prisoners in Italy and the withdrawal to the coasts of Italian troops in other countries. I sent for the political representatives and told them that General Castellano had never agreed to an 'unconditional surrender'. It was the Allied Governments and not the Italian Government who were now changing completely and fundamentally the obligations mutually undertaken and signed. It was a subterfuge which might have been forgiven had it been resorted to by a defeated nation in the hope of escaping too-heavy penalties, but it was ungenerous and dishonourable on the part of the victors with whom the defeated nation was now fully collaborating.

The resentment and the unhappiness which I showed immediately induced the Allied representatives to say that they had not drafted the document, and that in any case before I signed it I could discuss it during the meeting which I was shortly to have with General Eisenhower.

◆   ◆   ◆

Another very grave problem had to be settled during those days. Everywhere the German troops were committing horrible outrages against our troops and the civilian population. It was imperative to declare war on Germany so that our men who fell into the hands of the Germans should not be treated as *francs-tireurs* and shot. But another reason appeared to me as being of even greater importance: how could we prove to the British and Americans that we were really their allies and determined to fight beside them if we did not declare war on the common enemy? The answer to me was perfectly obvious, especially as first I, as Head of the Government, and then the King, had asked for an alliance. I therefore proposed to the King that he should declare war on the Germans, but he seemed doubtful. That evening the Minister to the Royal Household, who was himself opposed to the step, explained the reason to me; the King was afraid that the Germans, who were occupying five-sixths of Italy, would be infuriated and would carry out barbarous reprisals on the population. 'That is true,' I answered, 'it may happen, but we have taken the decisive step in changing our policy, and we cannot go back on that. Either the King will consent or I shall resign.'

I asked General Mason-MacFarlane, who was tactfully
urging such a declaration, for a little more time in which
to convince the King, being sure that I should succeed.
A few days afterwards Mason-MacFarlane allowed me to
see a document of the Allied Supreme Command, which
in the name of the Allied Governments laid down the
following points:

1. A state of co-belligerency with Italy will be recognized after that country has declared war on Germany.
2. The Government of Marshal Badoglio must continue in office.
3. The Allies will support with all means at their disposal the authority of the King and the Government
   without prejudice to the fact that after the expulsion
   of the Germans the people shall be free to choose the
   form of government they prefer.
4. As soon as possible Marshal Badoglio will broaden
   the basis of his government.
5. Possible modifications of the terms of the Armistice
   and the handing over of Italian territory will depend
   on the conduct of the Italian Government.
6. Instructions on political, financial, and economic
   questions will be transmitted as laid down in Article
   12 of the armistice.

As a matter of fact very few of these promises were carried
out.

General Mason-MacFarlane then told me that General
Eisenhower wished to have a meeting with me at Malta
on the morning of 19 September and it was arranged that
I should proceed in an Italian cruiser.

CHAPTER XI

Military Problems

THE Anglo-American strategy in Italy has been the subject of lively discussions and of not entirely justifiable criticism. This is not surprising, as amateur strategists have flourished in all ages and in all countries. Some, indeed a considerable number, of these amateurs blame the Allied High Command for not having carried out the landings to the north of Rome, but this criticism is lacking in substance for it ignores one vital factor. It was essential for the Allies to have constant and strong air cover at sea and on the beaches. This cover could not be provided by aircraft flown from carriers; it had to be reinforced by fighter planes from aerodromes in Sicily. These aircraft could not operate farther north than Naples and to ensure greater security Salerno was chosen for the landing as it offered suitable beaches.

It was not therefore a strategical blunder to choose Salerno. In my opinion the real and grave strategical error occurred at an earlier stage—it was the decision to seize Sicily. The occupation of that island, at the extreme south of Italy, involved the Allies, as they later found to their cost, in fighting their way up the whole length of the peninsula.

Their position would have been entirely different and they would have had a far larger zone of action had they chosen Sardinia. One glance at the map of Italy is enough to prove my contention. The occupation of Sardinia would not have presented greater naval and military difficulties to the Allies than that of Sicily, while their information services ought to have told them that there were fewer enemy forces in Sardinia than in Sicily. A landing between Civitavecchia and Leghorn would have seriously menaced the German lines of communication with southern Italy. And in Sardinia there were good aerodromes for use as bases for fighter aircraft.

But given the facts of the case, that is to say, the occupation of Sicily, even then one cannot say that the subsequent operations of the Allies were shining examples of the art of war. There was one capital strategic blunder and many mistakes in tactics. The famous commanders who conducted this campaign will forgive my criticisms.

The strategical blunder was the lack of co-ordination in the timing of the landing of the 8th Army under Montgomery in the extreme south of Calabria and the landing of the 5th Army under Clark at Salerno. As a result the 8th Army was too far from the 5th to be able to give it any support during the critical phase of the disembarkation, nor could the 8th Army hope to attract many enemy forces to its front, for the Germans were not so unwise as to send troops into a country so mountainous and so roadless as Calabria.

If General Eisenhower had adhered to 12 September as the date of the armistice and of the landing, or, better still, had it been 15 September, the 5th Army could have received adequate support from the 8th.

Once the decision to land at Salerno had been taken, a careful study of the terrain of the interior of the country (maps were not lacking) would have suggested what ought to have been done. It was not done or done very imperfectly, and the troops were forced to retreat almost to the beaches, where the terrible fire from the guns of the fleet stopped the German tanks.

Two causes slowed down the Allies. In the first place there was an almost overwhelming preoccupation to save the lives of their men—a justifiable preoccupation which concerned me all the time during the campaign in East Africa—but which must not be allowed to exceed certain limits, otherwise it is impossible to wage war at all. All the Americans repeated the same slogan—'It takes twenty years to make a man, and only a few hours to make a machine. So, send up the machines!'

The smallest obstacle held up the troops, and when this happened an immense number of guns with fantastic supplies of ammunition immediately began a bombardment which lasted for hours with very rapid if not very accurate fire on any inhabited centre or even a fold in the ground. It did not stop even when our peasants from the area that was being deluged with shells declared that there was no enemy near and offered to accompany the troops if they would advance. Naturally such expert fighters as the Germans immediately grasped the methods of attack used by their enemies and adapted their tactics to it. They never presented large targets, but organized small detachments with a single gun, or some machine-guns to attract the enemies' attention and fire, and then took up other positions.

The other factor which slowed up the advance was the over-mechanization of all units. Again even the most cursory study of the map would have proved that this complete motorization, however suitable to the Libyan desert, was quite unsuitable for the mountains of Italy. We had to remedy this defect, organizing many supply columns which rendered great services to the Allies. Finally, after the capture of Monte Marrone,[1] a feat which astonished everybody, a school for mountain warfare was established with officers from our Alpine regiments as instructors.

∾   ∾   ∾

[1] End of December 1943. A height near Naples. (*Translator.*)

The questions relating to our armed forces were of extreme difficulty and complexity. I will deal briefly with each.

As regards the Army: most of this was in northern Italy, which was occupied by the Germans, in France, in Croatia, in Montenegro, in Greece, and the Ionian Islands. By means of the Allied intelligence services we tried to send instructions to the troops in the Balkans and in Greece to join the Partisans, and we ordered the forces in the occupied areas in Italy to form guerrilla bands. We besought the Allied High Command to send reinforcements to our garrisons on the Ionian Islands, particularly in Cefelonia and Corfu, but the Allies replied that their own needs prevented them from detaching troops from other sectors, and our garrisons after a determined resistance were overwhelmed by the Germans.

The troops in the liberated provinces were formed into an army, but officers and men alike were bewildered and a subtle propaganda campaign tried to discredit our forces. In addition to the revivifying efforts of our High Command, I not only issued a manifesto to the soldiers, workers, and peasants, but I held many meetings of officers at which very quietly and clearly but with all the enthusiasm at my command, I explained why we were fighting beside the English and the Americans and the duty which was laid upon us, not to let the Allies, single-handed, free our country from the Germans. It was a question of honour and of life itself that we should play our part in this great enterprise. All this had the desired effect and very soon the morale of the troops was restored.

We also impressed on the Allies the necessity of protecting the islands of Sardinia, Corsica, and Elba, but there again we had to act alone. In the two larger islands the Germans were defeated and expelled by our troops, except for some slight help from the French in Corsica. Elba was seized by the Germans.

The rescue of our troops from the coasts of Dalmatia and Albania was particularly difficult, but even though we had no assistance we were able to transport thousands of our men to harbours in the Puglie. Of the remainder, some were taken prisoners by the Germans and some joined the 'Florentine', the 'Venetian', and the 'Turin' divisions and, led by experienced officers, fought side by side with the Partisans.

Our Navy, although it suffered heavy losses from German air attacks, carried out the armistice terms with complete loyalty and discipline. At the moment of writing[1] it is based partly at Malta and partly on North African ports, longing to be in action once again, an event which cannot be long postponed.

The Air Force, which even before the armistice was reduced to a mere handful owing to the enormous losses it had sustained, was gradually concentrated on the aerodromes in the Puglie; almost every day an aeroplane arrived, the pilot having escaped from the Germans to join our forces. Scraping together all the aircraft dispersed in Sicily and Sardinia, the Minister for Air, General Sandalli, was able to re-create an Air Force of about 350 machines which included bombers, fighters, and torpedo-bombers.

೨·   ೨·   ೨·

I have already given the text of my telegram to General Eisenhower asking that we might fight beside the Allies. I was allowed to organize a motorized force of 5,200 men which went into action at the beginning of December in

[1] The author gives no date, but this is clearly prior to 13 October 1943, when Italy declared war on Germany. (*Translator.*)

the zone of the American 5th Army. This force was gradually increased until it numbered 21,000 men and it was greatly praised for its achievements in mountain war-fare. But although we had been promised modern arms for several divisions we never received any.

As I have said, we furnished many supply columns which carried munitions and food up to the front lines, many divisions to protect the lines of communications, some technical formations, and more than 100,000 men who served in a 'Pioneer Corps', but *we were not allowed to increase our armed forces.*

I said we were not given arms: it would be more accurate to say that many were taken from us to be sent to the Balkans.

It was an extraordinary way to treat us. The Heads of the Allied Governments called on the Italians to increase their forces, suggesting that the mitigation of the terms of the armistice depended on the part we played in the war. At the same time the Allied Headquarters in Algiers and the Allied Command in Italy prevented, by every means in its power, our taking any share in the fighting.

⌁   ⌁   ⌁

As soon as co-belligerency was declared the Navy was treated as an Allied fleet. All the light craft and the cruisers (except five, three of which were later returned to us) took part in operations in the Mediterranean and the Atlantic, winning the admiration of the English and the Americans.

Our Air Force was at once used in the Balkan sector where it carried out not only many bombing raids and machine-gun attacks, but also took orders and supplies to our detachments fighting with the Partisans.

I repeatedly asked the Allies that our fine pilots should

be provided with modern planes; only at the beginning of May did we receive sufficient aircraft from the English to equip five squadrons, three of fighters and two of bombers.

More than once Mr. Churchill paid a warm tribute to the work of the Italian armed forces. Similar tributes came from the commanders of the Allied troops in Italy. Commendation, frequent praise—accompanied by an absolute ban on any increase of these armed forces!

Special care and thought was devoted to the reorganization of the Carabinieri Reali. This service was radically cleared of undesirable elements and new men enlisted. The task was carried out most successfully by General Piéche; more than 2,300 Carabinieri were taken to Rome by the Allies after the liberation of that city to carry out the important duties of military police.

CHAPTER XII

The Difficulties Increase

O N 28 September Mason-MacFarlane and I left Brindisi in the cruiser *Scipione l'Africano* with an escort of four destroyers.

When I arrived at Malta I was received on board the battleship *Nelson* with military honours; she was a magnificent ship with a very smart crew. I immediately saw General Eisenhower and his Chief of Staff, General Bedell Smith, whom I had already met at Brindisi; Lord Gort, the Governor of Malta, and General Alexander, commanding the Allied forces in Italy, were also present.

When General Eisenhower, Bedell Smith, Mason-MacFarlane, and I began our conference I opened the proceedings by asking General Eisenhower if he still regarded the armistice which he had signed on 3 September with my representative General Castellano, as being in force; he said yes, but that that armistice only contained military clauses, while the present document contained political and economic clauses. I replied that the new armistice had one radical difference in the military terms which had formerly been agreed upon. It spoke of 'unconditional surrender', while the first armistice simply dealt with the cessation of all hostilities in all theatres of war between the Italian and the British and American troops. I submitted the following points to him:

1. We had loyally executed all the conditions of the armistice of 3 September, suffering terrible losses owing to the tragic way in which the terms of the armistice had been implemented on the insistence of the British and Americans.

2. Nevertheless as soon as I arrived in Brindisi we had complied with all General Eisenhower's demands, as General Mason-MacFarlane could testify, and had collaborated to the fullest extent.

3. We had not committed any act which could justify the Allies in increasing the severity of the terms of the armistice.

4. The new document represented a complete change of policy, it was disadvantageous and humiliating to us, and we had not been informed of the reason for this change.

5. That Great Britain and the United States, as well as Italy, had undertaken solemn pledges at Cassibile.

General Mason-MacFarlane then said that he wished to speak to General Eisenhower and General Bedell Smith in private and these three adjourned to a nearby cabin. When they returned General Mason-MacFarlane said that they had not drawn up the new document but acting under orders from their Governments they were only concerned with presenting it to me for signature. He added that should I refuse to sign, the very gravest consequences would follow for in that event the Governments had decided to regard Italy simply as a defeated and partially occupied country, and would take immediate action accordingly. Both General Eisenhower and General Bedell Smith were obviously very much distressed; the latter even said that it would be easy to alter certain phrases, bringing the new armistice into line with the spirit of the armistice of 3 September.

General Eisenhower then said to me:

Marshal, I am very well acquainted with the whole of your military career and I know too what you have done for your country. Like you, I have noticed that there is an alteration in the military terms, but we are not responsible. General

Mason-MacFarlane has told you that if you do not sign, the result will be disastrous for Italy. I give you my word of honour as a soldier that I will do all in my power to change the wording of this present armistice as General Bedell Smith has said, and that in addition this document will remain absolutely secret.[1]

General Eisenhower spoke with such sincerity and feeling and his words conveyed such a determination to play his part loyally, that I was much moved. Not to sign meant fresh suffering for Italy and I was convinced that he meant what he said, and I signed. General Eisenhower kept his word.

◦ ◦ ◦

When the ceremony was over General Eisenhower handed me the following letter:

The terms of the armistice to which we have just appended our signatures are supplementary to the short military armistice signed by your representative and mine on the 3rd September 1943. They are based upon the situation obtaining prior to the cessation of hostilities. Developments since that time have altered considerably the status of Italy, which has become in effect a co-operator with the United Nations.

It is fully recognized by the Governments on whose behalf I am acting that these terms are in some respects superseded by subsequent events and that several of the clauses have become obsolescent or have already been put into execution. We also recognize that it is not at this time in the power of the Italian Government to carry out certain of the terms. Failure to do so because of existing conditions will not be regarded as a breach of good faith on the part of Italy. However, this document represents the requirements with which the Italian Government can be expected to comply when in a position to do so.

[1] For the text of this document and the subsequent alterations see *Documents relating to the Conditions of an Armistice with Italy (September–November 1943)*. H.M. Stationery Office. Cmd. 6693. (*Translator.*)

It is to be understood that the terms of this document and of the short military armistice of the 3rd September may be modified from time to time if military necessity or the extent of co-operation by the Italian Government indicates this as desirable.[1]

There followed a discussion during which General Eisenhower immediately raised the question of our declaring war on Germany. I replied that I wished to do this as soon as possible; we then reviewed the question of our military collaboration and Eisenhower promised to help us with regard to armaments.

In the afternoon I went with the Minister of Marine, De Courten, to visit our ships which were at anchor in a harbour a little distance away. It was with great emotion that I saw those splendid crews who had fought so bravely, and I made a cheerful speech to the officers, promising them to do everything in my power to see that they were in action again as soon as possible.

◇   ◇   ◇

At Brindisi General Mason-MacFarlane handed on to me a message from Count Sforza[2] which had been forwarded to him by the American Department of State. In this message Count Sforza asserted that it was the duty of every Italian to give unconditional support to the Government of Marshal Badoglio so that this might enjoy the confidence of the Allies, and that any attempt to embarrass its work would be a criminal act. He also declared that all internal questions should be examined and decided after the Germans had been driven out of Italy.

[1] Official text. *Documents*, &c., op. cit.
[2] Italian High Commissioner in Turkey, 1918–19; Senator, 1919; Under-Secretary for Foreign Affairs, 1919–20; Foreign Minister, 1920–1; Ambassador to France, 1922; resigned on advent of Fascism; left Italy, 1927; lived in France, 1927–40, when he went to the United States. (*Translator*.)

But shortly afterwards when Count Sforza arrived in Italy and came to see me at Brindisi, he informed me that while giving every support to my Government and being willing to undertake missions in England and more particularly in America, he could not join the Government as I had invited him to do. The price of his collaboration was that the King should abdicate, that the Crown Prince should renounce the throne, and that a regency should be set up for the Prince's son. I was to be the regent. It is obvious that this declaration bore little resemblance to his original message.

Apart from the opportuneness of such a grave act at so difficult a moment, it seemed to me that to force the King to abdicate and the Crown Prince to renounce his right to the throne, was not within my power, nor within the power of any other government, only the whole nation and not a fraction of it, as would be the case in the circumstances, had the right to express its will in so vital a matter. If I had acted as Sforza wished me to do, I should have been acting as a dictator and not as the head of a democratic government.

However I did not abandon hope. As General Mason-MacFarlane insisted that I should complete my Cabinet I went with him to Naples to confer again with Sforza and Croce,[1] but they insisted on a regency. I then had a meeting with Rodinò, the leader of the Christian-Democrat Party; he supported Sforza, informing me in addition that the six parties of the 'United Front' who had collaborated with me in Rome were agreed on this point. When I got back to Brindisi I assured Mason-MacFarlane that I had tried to form a government and that I had failed, therefore I should place my resignation in the hands of the King.

[1] Benedetto Croce, philsopher and Liberal politician. (*Translator.*)

In order that the King might be *au courant* with the situation I wrote him a letter of explanation.

At the same time Mason-MacFarlane left to take up a new appointment at Gibraltar; it was announced that he would be succeeded by the American General Joyce while General Taylor acted temporarily as Head of the Commission.

It seemed to me that the moment had come to induce the King to declare war on Germany. I therefore raised the question with him again; he agreed, and so on 13 October in his name I declared war on Germany and ordered our Ambassador in Madrid, Marchese Paolucci De' Calboli, to hand the declaration to the German Ambassador to Spain. I also ordered our Minister in Berne to ask the Swiss Government to take charge of our interests in Germany, Japan, and the occupied countries. The Swiss Government agreed and no Italian must ever forget all that they did for us.

General Joyce now arrived; he was the officer commanding an American cavalry division, a most sympathetic personality, kind and friendly, he found himself for the first time confronted by the complications of European politics. In the short period that he was with us he made himself very popular.

Following our declaration of war on Germany, the Allies announced that they regarded Italy as a co-belligerent. This meant that they recognized that we were fighting at their side against a common enemy. But to make clear the meaning of the word, they hurriedly declared that all the clauses of the armistice remained in force and that it was only by her conduct that Italy could obtain any mitigation of them. Churchill expressed this in a picturesque phrase when he said that 'Italy must work her passage.' As soon as co-belligerency was announced all our naval units (except the cruisers) joined the Allied Navies, flying the Italian flag, to take their part in escorting convoys and in naval actions in the Mediterranean and the Atlantic.

A special convention to deal with the situation was discussed, agreed, and signed by our Minister of the Navy, Admiral De Courten, and the Allied Commander-in-Chief in the Mediterranean, Admiral Cunningham. Our ships were at once fully employed, and carried out their duties so satisfactorily that the officers of the numerous convoys in the Mediterranean began to insist on the escorts being provided by Italian ships, as they thought them more vigilant than the British or the Americans.

It was our fate that no sooner had we made one step forward, after the greatest struggle, than we were immediately dragged back by the Allies.

General Joyce and Major Caccia, the English political officer, came to see me to present two new documents. The first contained the changes in the armistice signed in Malta; as a result of General Eisenhower's representations the Allied Governments had cancelled the phrase 'unconditional surrender' and substituted the title 'additional conditions of Armistice with Italy'. There remained, however, in Article I the phrase 'the surrender on the part of Italy', but the difference between the first and second armistices was less marked. The second document was an amendment, in a restrictive sense, of the agreement drawn up and signed by De Courten and Cunningham. Joyce and Caccia stated that they would not deliver the first document unless I signed the second.[1]

I was very angry. I said that I was being taken literally by the throat, in order to force me to sign the second document. Admiral De Courten had prepared a written pro-

---

[1] For official text see *Documents*, &c., op. cit.

test and I handed them the original, keeping a copy for myself.[1] 'You are the victors and we are the vanquished', I said to them, 'but when these documents are made public, history will describe them in fitting terms.'

I then wrote the following letter to Roosevelt and Churchill:

The armistice signed by my orders on 3 September by General Castellano did not contain any clause referring to the surrender of Italy. As you know, nearly all the clauses dealt with military matters. I was then told that other clauses dealing only with civil questions would be handed to me later.

On 29 September when we had loyally carried out all the terms of the armistice and when with the complete approval of the Anglo-American Commission the period of full co-operation had begun, I was obliged at Malta to sign additional clauses which altered and aggravated the terms of the armistice of 3 September, this later document being headed 'The Unconditional Surrender of Italy'.

As a result of my protests, General Eisenhower undertook to represent to the Allied Governments the reasons for my objections, and to propose the cancellation of the phrases especially and uselessly hurtful to the good name of Italy. In addition these were in my opinion prejudicial to the common cause which it is my firm intention to support by every means in my power.

On 27 October the Head of the Allied Commission assured me explicitly and formally in writing that the British, American, and Soviet Governments had approved the amendments to the document containing the terms of the second armistice which you desired.

However, notwithstanding the passage from co-operation to co-belligerency and the assurances given me, the document which has been presented to me partially corrected, still contains the words 'unconditional surrender' which did not appear in the original armistice.

[1] For official text see *Documents*, &c., op. cit

The same thing has happened with regard to the naval agreement.

On 23 September this was discussed exhaustively between Admiral Cunningham and Admiral De Courten and complete agreement was reached. Now after a month an amendment has been forwarded to me in which the promised cancellation in the armistice of the words which were the subject of my protest, is finally conceded. But this is made to depend on my accepting a further naval clause, dealing with a matter already settled, a clause which seriously worsens the position of Italy.

I have been compelled, I repeat, to sign this amendment. I hope, Mr. President, you will find a way of re-examining this on the basis of the modification which I have drawn up.

I am happy to state that during this period three-quarters of the Italian naval forces have co-operated with the Allied naval forces; that Italian troops have been fighting in Sardinia and Corsica against the Germans; that Italians are fighting under particularly hard and trying conditions in Croatia, Montenegro, and Greece at the side of the Greeks and the Yugoslavs; that Italians are fighting under desperate conditions in northern Italy and are sabotaging the lines of communication and supply.

I am also happy to state that in the liberated zone not only have we complied with all the Allied requests but we have also demanded that our troops should be allowed to take part in the liberation of our country, a request which has been partially granted.

I believe that my Government in its temporary form provides, as far as possible in the present circumstances, those guarantees of law and order which it is in our and your interests to maintain. As you know this Government will be replaced as soon as we reach Rome by another more fully representative of the New Italy which has had to struggle into existence in a country torn by war and facing many internal troubles. My Government therefore feels great bitterness over the incessant and constant worsening of conditions already discussed and agreed with the Allied Governments.

I

We are uncertain of our position; we are deprived of communications, of any means of receiving information from the outside world, of direct contact with the tens of millions of Italians resident in other countries, and with our diplomatic representatives abroad. We lack those fundamental elements of liberty which we intend to foster in the interests of our country.

It is for this reason, Mr. President, that I address myself to you personally because the Italian nation is faced with many grave and tragic difficulties; because of the firm determination of myself and my Government to fight by your side against the common enemy; because of my determination to give my country those liberal institutions which are your strength. As you are undoubtedly among the greatest and most honoured upholders of those criteria of human justice, you will take all these circumstances into account in deciding your action towards Italy.

If the changes in the armistice had been dictated by the desire to give Italy and her Government greater opportunities of employing her forces and her supplies in the common struggle for the liberation of the country from the Germans, the aggravation of the burdens laid on her which such changes involved, would not only have been justified but would have been welcomed. Instead, the terms of the armistice of 29 September and the successive protocols and amendments and above all the manner in which they were interpreted and enforced by the Allied Commission of Control, frustrated in many instances the endeavours of the Italian Government to hasten the triumph of the Allied cause.

⋄   ⋄   ⋄

Meanwhile, calling on men of goodwill, who put the desire to serve Italy before everything else, I managed to form a Ministry. Some of its members were old parliamentarians who had never been Fascists, others were experts. I did not for the moment announce the resignation of the Government created on 26 July in Rome so the new members were appointed as under-secretaries.[1]

Piccardi, the Minister of Industry and Commerce, had already resigned in order to join the Army.

At the same time the Allied Commission of Control (the successor to the original Allied Mission) arrived and its members were attached to every Ministry in order to assist us. I shall have more to say later of the activities of the new Ministry and of the Allied Commission of Control.

The liberty of the press was restored with only the necessary military censorship. As had been foreseen, innumerable papers sprang into existence, their number being limited only by the scarcity of newsprint. They represented every shade of opinion expressed in terms of the greatest violence with very little appeal to reason. However, little by little, as the result of good sense and of Allied intervention, the press became more dignified.

◦⌒   ◦⌒   ◦⌒

The Allied military operations did not proceed with the speed which we had expected. Naples had been liberated; its courageous population which had stoically borne 120

[1] By the Order in Council of 16 November 1943 the resignation of Dr. Leopoldo Piccardi as Minister of Industry, Commerce, and Labour was accepted. By another Order in Council of the same date the following were appointed Under-Secretaries of State by the Head of the Government: Internal Affairs, Dr. Vito Reale; Justice, Dr. Giuseppe De Santis; Finance, Guido Jung; War, General Taddeo Orlando; Mercantile Marine, Admiral Pietro Barone; Education, Professor Giovanni Cuomo; Public Works, Professor Raffaele De Caro; Agriculture and Forests, Professor Tommaso Siciliani; Industry, Commerce, and Labour, Professor Epicarmo Corbino; Railways and Road Transport, General Giovanni Di Raimondo; Post and Telegraphs, Professor Mario Fano.

bombings, did not stand idle but rose furiously against the Germans and there were several days of street-fighting.

The Germans were flung back across the Volturno to the Garigliano. In the Adriatic sector Foggia was occupied and the advance continued to the Trigno.

Accompanied by the Chief of the General Staff, I went to see General Alexander at S. Spirito. The meeting took place in an atmosphere of mutual confidence and it was agreed that as soon as it was ready an Italian contingent should be sent to the Tyrrhenian front to serve with the American 5th Army which was operating in that sector. The 8th British Army was in the Adriatic sector under General Montgomery. General Alexander invited us to send a small number of liaison officers to serve on his staff. He told me that he needed another three weeks (it was 6 October) to organize his supplies of ammunition and his depots after which he would launch a heavy attack.

But the results of this offensive did not correspond to the hopes that had been entertained; in the Tyrrhenian sector General Clark with the 5th Army made limited advances but did not reach the famous 'Gustav' line which the Germans had established at Cassino. Our forces took part in the fighting, but as a result of causes over which they had no control, could not carry out the task allotted to them, although they fought bravely and suffered considerable losses.

In the Adriatic sector which consisted of a series of parallel ridges a few miles apart and separated by streams pompously known as 'rivers' (as small towns are called 'cities'),[1] the advance of the 8th Army, given its immense superiority in weapons, was slowly methodical. The impressive quantity of supplies disembarked and the immense dumps of munitions and petrol which lined the roads for

[1] i.e. in Italy. (*Translator*.)

mile after mile had roused the greatest enthusiasm and convinced everyone that the German resistance would be pulverized and Rome liberated almost at once. But this enthusiasm faded into disappointment and discouragement.

CHAPTER XIII

The Government extends its Jurisdiction

DURING December a few German planes bombed the port of Bari at night. As there had not been any other air attacks in Puglia the fear of raids had practically disappeared and so had the air-raid precautions. At that moment there were about thirty steamers in port, some loaded with ammunition, others with petrol, and nearly all of them were tied up alongside each other to facilitate unloading. The attackers came in from the sea unobserved, indeed, the anti-aircraft batteries only opened fire when the bombs had begun to fall. Some of them hit the centre of the town causing casualties among the civilian population and destroying a certain number of buildings. The chief weight of the attack, however, was on the harbour, where additional damage was done by the ammunition blowing up and by the fires in the tankers. In all twenty-four ships were sunk. The Germans did not realize the havoc they had wrought and hardly mentioned the raid in their wireless bulletins, but as a matter of fact it was one of the most successful of their attacks.

It made a great impression on the Allied Mission which was housed in the International Hotel at Brindisi, just opposite the quays. The port was always full of shipping and the work of unloading went on night and day; in addition the quays were piled high with ammunition and bombs. General Joyce immediately gave orders for these to be moved to safer localities, but this took about a month. The Mission therefore decided to go and sleep in a village in the Salentine peninsula, returning each morning to

Brindisi. This meant that four hours a day were lost in going backwards and forwards.

General Joyce told me that it was considered essential that the Government should be moved elsewhere. He decided on Sorrento, but when he visited that locality he found out that it was entirely occupied by Allied hospitals. Salerno was chosen, although there too most of the buildings were in the possession of the Allies. I made it a condition of the transfer that the province should be put under Italian administration, and that proper accommodation was provided for me.

      ◇   ◇   ◇

Meanwhile it was announced that General Eisenhower was expected and it was arranged that I should meet him and General Alexander at S. Spirito, near Bari. Some time previously Marshal Messe and Generals Orlando and Berardi had been released, and General Ambrosio, who had already passed the retiring age, spontaneously suggested to me that he should be succeeded by Marshal Messe as Chief of the General Staff. I obtained the King's approval and appointed Ambrosio Inspector-General of the Army. I chose Orlando as Minister of War and Berardi as Chief of the Army General Staff; he took the place of Roatta who had been charged by the Yugoslavs with acts of cruelty when he was in command of an army on the eastern front—a charge so far unsubstantiated.

At the conference Marshal Messe began by making the very strongest protest against the Allied demand that we should send arms and ammunition to the Balkan partisans. Neither General Eisenhower nor General Bedell Smith knew anything of this, and when General Bedell Smith had read the Allied demand, he exclaimed: 'We want the Italians to fight beside the Allies against the Germans and in order to improve their morale, we take away their arms!' The demand was immediately withdrawn. Our collaboration was then discussed and it was at once agreed that we should be given the equipment of one division, the arms for another two divisions, and the tools and machinery necessary for the organization of numerous technical units. None of these promises was fulfilled.

After the meeting was over General Bedell Smith asked to speak to me alone; he told me that he was giving up his present appointment as he had been transferred to another post. He said that he was happy and proud to have known me and to have been able to collaborate with me. I thanked him, assuring him of my warm regard and wishing him every success in his new appointment. In my opinion General Bedell Smith was the ablest officer on the Allied Supreme Command; among the Allied officers in Italy he was famous for his drive. I always found him most sympathetic and generous to us. If he could not do more for us it was because he had to carry out the orders he had received. I am very glad of this opportunity to express my friendship and admiration for General Bedell Smith.

The Allies had set up a Consultative Commission for Italian affairs; it consisted of one representative each from Great Britain, the United States, Russia, France, Greece, and Yugoslavia. General Joyce asked me to go with him to Naples to be present at the first meeting of the Commission. On that occasion M. Massigli, the French representative, was in the chair and he asked me to make a statement on Italy's collaboration in the war.

I began by saying that I was sure (though privately I very much doubted it) that the Commission would immediately invite an Italian representative to take part in its proceedings. I underlined that although its members represented the very highest level of theoretical knowledge and intelligence, the lack of an Italian—who could contribute specialized knowledge and experience of Italian affairs and psychology—was an obvious gap, which should be filled as soon as possible. Going on to talk of the contribution spontaneously made by Italy, I gave a clear account of what we had done in the military field to increase and support our fighting forces. I recalled all the promises to provide us with arms, promises which had never been fulfilled, the limitations continually imposed on our co-operation, and the confiscation of our arms for the benefit of the Balkan partisans. I concluded with some heat: 'I am asked what is, and what could be, our contribution to the Allied cause, but I have something to ask you—am I sitting as this table as a friend or an enemy?'

M. Vishinsky, the Russian representative, assured me that I was regarded as a friend. M. Massigli said that the question of an Italian member had not been discussed and that even the functions of the Commission had not been laid down. At the end of the sitting M. Vishinsky told me that the Soviet Government wished to see Italy liberated as soon as possible, and once again a strong and prosperous country. He added (as he had already told Prunas) that the Soviet Government was anxious to establish direct relations with the Italian Government. I thanked him for what he had said about Italy and said that I shared his desire for direct relations between our two Governments. I immediately repeated the substance of this conversation to General Joyce. I shall explain later the developments and unforeseen repercussions of this discussion.

◦᷿◦   ◦᷿◦   ◦᷿◦

On 6 January General Joyce was recalled to America and General Mason-MacFarlane returned. He told me that his headquarters would be in Naples and that he wanted to have under his control not only A.M.G.O.T. but all the Allied services so that there might be unity of direction and action. He also informed me that when my Government moved to Salerno the Allies intended to hand over the administration of all the provinces south of Naples and Foggia, excluding the islands of Pantelleria and Lampedusa. This transfer, however, depended on our acceptance of certain conditions of which he gave me a written statement.

I replied, also in writing, that these conditions raised many important and complicated questions, and that I had nominated a committee consisting of Jung, the Under-Secretary of Finance, Innocenti, the Chief of the Cabinet Office, and Professor Forti, an administrative expert, which would forward their comments and proposals. In the meanwhile, however, I pointed out that the islands excluded from the concession were purely Italian and that I could not understand their exclusion except for military considerations, arising from a state of war. I did not receive any answer to this communication.

The committee quickly finished its work; it suggested many amendments, which we regarded as essential, but they were not agreed to. We had no further choice in the matter if we were to exercise even a limited authority over the provinces, and repair the damage which the Allied administration had done by adopting different methods and regulations in the different provinces. Thanks to the energetic intervention of General Mason-MacFarlane with the Allied territorial authorities at Salerno, most of the remaining obstacles to the transfer were overcome.

Contemporaneously with the return of the southern

provinces and the other islands, the Government was re-organized to give it the necessary standing and prestige *vis-à-vis* the other nations. The Ministers who found it impossible to carry out their duties as they had remained in territory occupied by the enemy, were relieved of their posts, and the King was thus able to make new appointments. The composition of the Cabinet remained practically unchanged because in nearly every case the under-secre-taries were given the rank of Minister. The President of the Court of Cassation who was in liberated territory, became Lord Privy Seal however, and Signor Lucifero became Minister of Agriculture. A few days previously Signor Philipson, who had given me most valuable assis-tance since the early days at Brindisi, had been made Under-Secretary in the Cabinet Office.[1]

[1] Owing to the circumstances of the moment the following ministers were unable to carry out their duties, and so on the advice of the Head of the Government the King revoked their appointments by an Order in Council, dated 11 February 1944: Dr. Raffaele Guariglia, Minister of Foreign Affairs; Dr. Umberto Ricci, Minister of Internal Affairs; Dr. Bartolini, Minister of Finance; General Antonio Sorice, Minister of War; Dr. Leonardo Severi, Minister of Education; Dr. Antonio Romano, Minister of Public Works; Senator Alessandro Brizi, Minister of Agriculture and Forests; General Frederico Amoroso, Minister of Communications. By an Order in Council of the same date, the King on the advice of the Head of the Government, appointed the following ministers: Foreign Affairs, Marshal Pietro Badoglio; Interior, Dr. Vito Reale; Finance, Guido Jung; War, General Taddeo Orlando; Education, Professor Giovanni Cuomo; Public Works, Dr. Raffaele De Caro; Agriculture and Forests, Dr. Falcone Luci-fero; Communications, Dr. Tommaso Siciliani; Industry, Commerce, and Labour, Professor Epicarmo Corbino. By an Order in Council of 15 Feb-ruary the King, on the advice of the Head of the Government and for the same reason, revoked the appointment of the Minister of Justice, Dr. Gaetano Azzariti, and accepted the resignation of Dr. Giuseppe De Santis as Under-Secretary in the same Ministry. By an Order in Council of the same date the King, on the advice of the Head of the Government, appointed as Minister of Justice Dr. Ettore Casati. Dr. Dino Philipson had been appointed an Under-Secretary in the Cabinet Offices on 1 February, while by an Order in Council of 24 February Professor Pietro Capasso was appointed Under-Secretary for Internal Affairs.

There were rumours that General Alexander was considering a new landing and these were confirmed by the fact that Naples, Castellamare, and Salerno were crowded with landing-craft. It was said that the operation would coincide with a heavy attack by the 5th Army on the defensive line at Cassino.

The hope of liberating Rome revived. The American officers at Naples were wildly excited. I soon heard all about the plan. The landing was to take place in the area of Anzio and Nettuno and was to be made by three divisions; my heart fell. Three divisions were entirely inadequate to protect the beachhead and to advance in depth to threaten German communications. The landing was a complete surprise to the German High Command, the beaches were in Allied hands but the troops were fully occupied in defending them and were not in sufficient strength to carry out further operations. The Germans reacted violently, launching furious attacks; there followed days of great anxiety lest the Allies should be thrown back into the sea. The losses on both sides were heavy and the Allies had to rush up reinforcements.

At the same time the Air Forces dropped more than 2,000 tons of bombs on Cassino and after a terrific artillery bombardment, which lasted for several hours, the infantry attacked. But they were held up by well-directed fire and hardly any ground was gained. The bright hopes of the first days were followed by disappointment and discouragement.

I was told that the American General Donovan, a close friend of President Roosevelt's, was at Naples. I had known him at Buffalo in 1924 and I had seen him again in 1936 at Macallè in Abyssinia where he had come to report on the situation for President Roosevelt. He sent me a message to say that he would have liked to come and see me but he could not leave Naples, so I went there and found that he had just returned from Anzio. I naturally told him all about my difficulties and he insisted that I should write to Roosevelt. In this letter I begged the President to take the initiative in bringing about a change in the political status of Italy and proposed an alliance.

      ◇   ◇   ◇

The real leaders of the political parties composing the 'United Front' were still in Rome but their representatives in the liberated territory were gradually giving more and more support to the views of Sforza and Croce. They asked the American authorities in Naples for permission to hold a congress in that city in which delegates from the provinces could take part. When the authorities refused, they sent a telegram of protest to Churchill and he replied that they could hold their congress in Bari. While pointing out that Bari was in territory under the control of the Italian Government, and therefore it would be for me and not for Mr. Churchill to give the necessary permission, I did not raise any objection to the congress being held. I only laid down that there should be no demonstrations in the streets so as to avoid the danger of disorder. I took the necessary security measures and assured the Allies that the law and order in this important Allied base would not be disturbed.

The congress took place in the theatre on 28 and 29 January. There were representatives of the Liberals, the Christian Democrats, of the Parties of Action, of Democracy, of Labour, of the Socialists, and the Communists. Many speeches were made, the proceedings were both lively and inconclusive, while abuse of every kind was hurled at the King, the Crown Prince, and the

Government. When it was over everyone went home in an orderly fashion.

৹·   ৹·   ৹·

During the winter there was an outbreak of typhus in Naples. I had had to deal with a similar outbreak in Venezia Tridentina in December 1918 after the return of the prisoners from Russia, and so I knew the seriousness of such an epidemic. In a city like Naples, with its enormous population living in most unhygienic conditions owing to the lack of water and the means of cleanliness, I was afraid that there would be a terrible mortality rate. The Allied authorities, however, organized the fight against the disease with a rapidity and efficiency which was really amazing. The city authorities, and particularly our doctors, also flung themselves into the fight with the greatest zeal. The result of the measures taken was immediately obvious. After a few days the number of cases and of deaths fell rapidly and in a short time the epidemic was mastered.

৹·   ৹·   ৹·

The Government was established and working efficiently at Salerno, the Control Commission was partly at Salerno and partly at Naples, when Churchill made a speech on Italian affairs in the House of Commons.[1] The British Prime Minister, after paying a warm tribute to the achievements of the Italian Army, Navy, and Air Force, declared that my Government had entirely satisfied the Allies in what we had done, and he doubted whether any other Government would enjoy an equal ascendency over the armed forces. Churchill added that he did not think it desirable to demand changes in the present Government.

[1] 21 September 1943. (*Translator.*)

The examination of the political situation in Italy and the question of forming a Government on a broader basis should be postponed till after the liberation of Rome. But even then he doubted whether the new Government would enjoy the same prestige with the armed forces.

The confidence shown by the Allied nations in handing over the southern provinces to the Italian Government and the praises of Churchill in the House of Commons undoubtedly increased the standing of the Government, and enabled it to devote itself with the greatest energy to the solution of the internal problems of the country.

By their demands for the abdication of the King and the renunciation of the succession by the Crown Prince, the leaders of the six parties found themselves in an impasse from which there seemed no way of escape. As I shall explain later, the intervention of the head of the Communist Party, Palmiro Togliatti, who with my consent had returned from Moscow, where he had spent ten years. provided a solution.

CHAPTER XIV

The Pact with Russia: Roosevelt's Declaration

As I have already explained, M. Vishinsky and I had agreed that it was desirable to establish direct relations between the Soviet and Italian Governments. I received reports from Sicily and Sardinia that Vishinsky had expressed warm sympathy for our country during talks with the military authorities. He had also declared that Italy should recover her former strength and should resume her historic role in the Mediterranean. But shortly after our meeting at Naples Vishinsky left for Moscow to take up an important appointment, and I was sure that he would become absorbed in pressing problems and would forget our conversation. I was entirely mistaken.

He was succeeded on the Commission by Ambassador Bogomolof. Asking for an interview, he reminded me of my conversation with Vishinsky and wished to know whether I was ready to put in writing the request to the Soviet Government to accredit a representative to the Italian Government, and for that Government to send a representative to Moscow. I told Bogomolof that I was always ready to confirm in writing anything I had stated verbally, and at once complied with his request.

In order to behave with the complete loyalty and correctness I had always observed in my relations with General Mason-MacFarlane, I told Prunas, the Secretary-General for Foreign Affairs, to see the Chief of the Control Commission immediately and to remind him of the communication I had made to General Joyce, and to give him all particulars of my interview with Bogomolof.

A few days later Bogomolof came to see me again accompanied by M. Kostilev and told me that Marshal Stalin had acceded to my request and had appointed M. Kostilev as his representative to the Italian Government. M. Kostilev was the First Councillor in the Soviet Embassy in Ankara and would be raised to the rank of Minister. I did not at the moment mention the name of an Italian representative to be sent to Moscow; Signor Quaroni, our Minister at Kabul, was eventually chosen. Bogomolof and I drafted the communiqué to be issued to the press. On the same day I sent Prunas to inform General Mason-MacFarlane.

The Anglo-American reaction was most unexpected. General Mason-MacFarlane came to see me and deplored that on this occasion I had not given him full information on such a grave question, not showing the frankness and sincerity which had always obtained between us. I immediately pointed out to him that he could not make such an accusation, because I had been most careful not only to inform General Joyce of my conversation at Naples with Vishinsky, but I had sent Prunas to tell him of the interview with Bogomolof. I said that up to the present my relations had been limited to two of the three Governments with whom I had signed the armistice, and I thought that it was only natural that I should wish to have direct relations with the third as soon as possible. I pointed out that not only was it in the interest of Italy to be in direct touch with such a great European Power as Russia had now become, but there were more than 70,000 Italian prisoners in that country and I longed for news of them. 'Even you, General,' I added, 'if you were in my position, would not have refused the first sign of friendship from one of the victorious Powers!'

Two days later General Mason-MacFarlane came to see

K

me again to bring me a letter which stated that by order
of the Supreme Allied Command the Italian Government
could not enter directly into relations with any Power,
allied or neutral. All communcations must be forwarded
through the Commission of Control for reasons of military
security.

This last statement put me on the 'black list' of suspected
persons and made me very angry. I sent General Mason-
MacFarlane the following communication:

I do not believe, my dear General, that the conditions of the
armistice, harsh though they may be, prohibit me from con-
cluding agreements with allied or neutral powers. Nor do I
believe that the Allied Supreme Command 'in the interest of
military security' is justified in its interference when such
security reasons cannot be defined or invoked.

This prohibition is therefore a further example of the
aggravation of the terms of the armistice, or at best, a more
restrictive interpretation of its clauses.

It is not justified by the attitude of myself or my Government towards the Allied Powers, nor particularly with reference to the recent Soviet initiative which provoked your
memorandum of 25 March. That initiative was, and is, a
friendly gesture towards Italy which I could not reject even
had I desired to do so. I must say quite frankly that this
method is nothing but a slow and progressive process of
asphyxiation. The Allied Administration does not limit itself
to supervising Italian administration and methods of government, but interferes in the smallest details of the life of the
country, and makes categorical and irrevocable decisions. I
and my Government are reduced to being simply an instrument
for carrying out Allied demands, while the country holds us
responsible for actions in which we have no part.

No Government, however it was constituted, could for long
continue to function within these progressively humiliating,
and above all, sterile limitations. I do not say that it would be
better, but it would at least be more honest and above board,

if the Allied Administration, wishing really to govern the country, decided to do so by direct methods and without this subterfuge.

I do not believe—though sometimes I am compelled to doubt—that this is really what you propose. So I must say, both loyally and with much friendship, my dear General, that to avoid such a grave situation at such a grave moment, it would be kind and wise in the interests of us all, if the Allies would initiate a policy that was really and definitely constructive.

You know, for example, that the word co-belligerency is an empty formula merely appearing in the armistice. You know besides that many causes of the armistice of 3 and 29 September are considered obsolescent, either because they have been carried out, or because it is impossible to execute them, or because they have been superseded by other agreements, &c.

Now I ask myself and I ask you if it would not be, as I firmly believe it would, far better for us and all concerned, if these documents were consolidated into a new agreement without the obsolescent clauses? Co-belligerency which we have most loyally practised for six months would then be clearly defined, on the basis that is to say of Italy's international status, and on what is today the real and effective state of affairs.

I do not think that I am asking the impossible.

I may blame myself for many mistakes, but at least I never failed in frankness and plain speaking in my dealings with the Allies. I believe that the matter was settled in some such way, and as a matter of fact the letter from Mason-MacFarlane was pigeon-holed.

But the English were still annoyed. The American and British Governments hastened to appoint Kirk and Charles[1] as representatives accredited to the Italian

[1] Sir Noel Charles, Bt., member of diplomatic service; Counsellor in Rome, 1937–8; Minister in Rome, 1939–40; Minister in Lisbon, 1940–1; Ambassador in Brazil, 1941–4; Ambassador in Italy, July 1944. (*Translator.*)

Government, without allowing me to send representatives to Washington and London.

Sir Noel Charles showed much sympathy and understanding for our country and in the course of a conversation I had with him, referred to our relations with Russia and the exchange of representatives between the two Governments. He told me that this had produced a coldness in Anglo-Italian relations; I answered that I did not understand why the British Government had taken up this matter only with me, and had not protested to Moscow.

⌁   ⌁   ⌁

My relations with Kostilev did not begin too happily. He told me that Marshal Stalin declared that the Yugoslav elements serving compulsorily in our armed forces were treated as slaves. Kostilev also believed that it was essential to send reinforcements to Marshal Tito and, therefore, he considered that I ought to allow a representative of the Marshal's to visit our formations and to draft all Yugoslavs to the Balkans.

This Yugoslav question had already given me a great deal of trouble. The English had brought thousands of Slav and Slovene refugees from the Dalmation coast to Italy. They were not very desirable guests; many wore red berets adorned with the hammer and sickle, and they were responsible for a series of outrages on the civilian population. I had had to have them collected in internment camps with the promise that as soon as possible they would be sent to North Africa. But many of them were engaged in underground activities. With the help of some Allied officials they had infiltrated into our armed forces to carry out a propaganda for desertion among our Slovene soldiers. Indeed a number of these had left their units, attracted by the promises of these agents. I protested with immediate success to General Mason-MacFarlane, giving the names of the deserters and of those who had rejoined their units. He was extremely annoyed at what had been happening and promised me that transport would quickly be provided for the Yugoslavs, and that immediate steps would be taken to put a stop to these undesirable activities. As a result the propaganda gradually came to an end.

M. Kostilev now raised the question on a legal basis. I answered in writing that I indignantly denied Marshal Tito's statement on the treatment of Slavs in our armed forces, and invited him to produce evidence in support of his allegations. I pointed out to M. Kostilev that the Slovenes serving in the ranks of the Italian Army were Italian subjects because they were inhabitants of territory within the frontiers of the Italian kingdom, as agreed with the Yugoslav Government in the Treaty of Rapallo. They were, therefore, called up for service under Italian law and in common with all other Italian subjects. If M. Kostilev was referring to them and asking me to hand them over to Marshal Tito to increase his forces, the request was absolutely inacceptable and contrary to our laws. If, however, M. Kostilev believed that we had conscripted Slavs who were not Italian subjects, I would point out that the inhabitants of the province of Ljubljana, annexed by Mussolini, had been exempted from military service. I was ready to agree to a commission appointed by General Mason-MacFarlane consisting of three members—an Englishman, an American, and a Russian—to visit our armed forces and to prove the truth of my statement.

Here the matter ended and the commission was not appointed. When I discussed the matter with General Mason-MacFarlane he told me that Marshal Tito was not in need of men but simply of munitions and food.

Another question arose at this moment which touched us even more nearly.

A Reuter telegram broadcast by the B.B.C. reported that President Roosevelt had stated at a press conference, that according to an agreement reached at Teheran, a third of the Italian fleet would be handed over to Russia, and that these ships, with Russian crews and flying the Red Flag, would be used outside the Mediterranean. This news spread like wildfire, as bad news always does, and aroused the greatest alarm in the country as well as the most vehement agitation among the crews. I immediately instructed the Minister of Marine to assure the officers and men that I was dealing with the matter and that they must remain calm. I begged General Mason-MacFarlane to come and see me; I told him that I had no official information as to whether this Reuter message was true, but if it were, my Government would resign at once as a protest. I assured him that no other Government would take office if such unwarranted action were taken. I pointed out that ever since the armistice our Navy had loyally carried out the pledges I had given but in such circumstances I could not undertake that the crews would not sink their ships wherever they might be, as a last and decisive protest against the action which Roosevelt had announced. General Mason-MacFarlane, who was both surprised and distressed, begged me not to take any action until there was an official communication from the Allied Governments, and not to make any statement to the press. I at once agreed to this most reasonable suggestion, but I warned him that in the afternoon I had to go to the King to put him in touch with the situation and to inform him of the decision of the Government.

A few days later an official American communiqué stated that the Reuter message was incorrect and that the correspondent in reporting the President's statement had omitted one phrase which entirely altered its meaning. Not one-third of the Italian fleet, but the equivalent in material, had been promised to Russia for operations in the Arctic by the British and Americans. The affair, more or less elegantly hushed up, was buried in oblivion.

But the resolute attitude of the Government produced an excellent impression in Italy and even the parties hostile to the Government sent me messages of support and approval.

CHAPTER XV

The New Provinces: The Allied Control Commission: The Elimination of Fascism

AMONG the provinces handed over to Italian administration on 11 February, the one which caused me the most anxiety was Sicily.

Signor Finocchiano Aprile had organized a movement which aimed at separating the island from the mother country and placing it under foreign protection. At the same time it was being openly said that the great landed proprietors were once again supporting the Mafia. Under Fascism, thanks to the energetic measures adopted by the prefect, Mori, that secret society had lost practically all its power. I saw a great many leading Sicilians who gave me very disquieting accounts of the state of affairs; even the more moderate thought that the only remedy was to grant a very large measure of local autonomy. The Government found the greatest difficulty in dealing with the situation owing to the precariousness of communications.

The question was debated at length in the Council of Ministers and it was decided that it was essential to appoint a High Commissioner with plenary powers. But in order not to revive the dictatorial methods of the Allies, the High Commissioner was to be assisted by a consultative committee consisting of nine members to be chosen by the Government. The High Commissioner would be present at the meetings of the Council of Ministers when Sicilian affairs were discussed, and he would submit proposals and report the views of the consultative committee. In this way the Government would be in close

touch with Sicilian problems and would be directly responsible for all decisions.

As Colonel Poletti had left Sicily to become Governor
of Naples and Campania, I consulted him as to the choice
of his successor. He suggested Musotto, as did the prominent Sicilians whom I also consulted. The Council of
Ministers was very much divided, but eventually agreed
to his appointment. Accompanied by the Minister of
Internal Affairs I flew to Palermo to instal him as High
Commissioner. On the following day I went to Catania,
where life had become almost normal, thanks to the energy
of the inhabitants, and then to Messina. I had seen that
city after it had been almost entirely destroyed by the
earthquake in 1908, and I had seen it many times while
it was being slowly and laboriously rebuilt. Now, thirty-
six years later, I saw it again when it had been almost
wiped out by bombing, more than 70 per cent. of its
houses having been destroyed.

As the most urgent need in Sicily appeared to be the
restoration of law and order which was threatened by
every form of crime, I ordered that the number of the
Carabinieri should be increased, and that those already
quartered in the island should be reorganized. At the
same time I arranged with General Mason-MacFarlane
to send two divisions of troops.

The Council of Ministers was not satisfied with the work
of the High Commissioner who was lacking in drive and
was not dealing effectively with the disorder in the island.
My Government decided to supersede him, and this was
done by the succeeding Government.

In Sardinia the chief problem was the reduction of the
large number of troops which had been collected there in
1943, still more having been brought from Corsica after
the successful liberation of that island. These men had to

be fed by the local population and were a heavy burden.
The Allies came to our help by supplying them with
rations, and then, as shipping became available, detachments were sent to Sicily and the mainland. In view of
the difficulty of communications it was again decided to
appoint a High Commissioner, and General of the Air
Force Pinna was chosen. He was himself a Sardinian and
much respected and loved by the inhabitants.

෴   ෴   ෴

I must now say something about the activities of the
Allied Control Commission. As will be remembered, a few
days after the Moscow Conference General Eisenhower
published a communiqué in which he announced the
formation of the 'A.C.C.'.

The Commission has control of the military and economic
activities of Italy as envisaged in the terms of the armistice.
Italy has a new role in the war; that is to fight the common
enemy, Germany. The Control Commission will see that all of
Italy's economic resources and manpower are utilized where
they can do most good in that fight. . . .
The United Nations are converting Italy into an effective
instrument of war against Germany. . . . They look to the
Italian Government to hasten the redemption of its country
and prove its value to the United Nations. . . .[1]

I must point out that Italy's new role in the war, that
is, of fighting against the Germans, was not assumed as the
result of the terms of the armistice, or of the Moscow Conference, or in virtue of agreements with the Allied Powers.
It was the unilateral decision of the Italian Government
following the spontaneous revolt of the people and the
armed forces after the publication of the armistice on

[1] Official translation. For full text see the *New York Times*, 11 November 1943. (*Translator.*)

8 September 1943. Therefore the Allied Control Commission ought to have been inspired by a desire to help Italy to play her part as a co-belligerent. What happened was exactly the opposite. To begin with, the title chosen for the committee was most unfortunate and did not contribute to the prestige of the Italian Government either at home or abroad.

The A.C.C. had but one preoccupation—to apply the terms of the armistice as severely and as extensively as possible. What ought, according to Eisenhower's communiqué, to have been 'a control of military and economic activities' became a rapidly increasing interference in all the details of Italian life, even in the political sphere. A political section of A.C.C. was immediately set up. The various sub-commissions began not only to 'control' but to issue their own orders, even one against the other. It is a well-known fact that all bureaucratic organisms have a natural tendency to expand so as to justify their existence and increase their importance.

All this, added to the regulations emanating from the military authorities (in practice independent of A.C.C.) as well as those devised by the Allied Military Government, made it impossible for the Italian Government to mobilize the forces of the nation so as to increase their contribution to the fight against Germany. Even in the provinces under Italian administration the most junior Allied officials could suspend or cancel the measures adopted by the highest Italian authority!

However, the very best relations and the most complete collaboration always existed between the President of the Allied Control Commission and myself. Some of the personnel were experienced and capable and approached their duties in the right spirit, but others were lacking in training and did not understand their duties. They found themselves unexpectedly invested with authority over millions of people in an unknown country in the midst of a crisis which had disorganized its social and economic life. When their activities did not produce the results they expected, the tendency of these officials was to accuse the Italians of being incompetent, lazy, and inefficient. They did not recognize the fact that their instructions had been issued without any understanding of customs and traditions which dated back for over two thousand years, and that they were dealing with a nation passing through the greatest trial of its history. As for their accusations of laziness and inefficiency, the world knows how much the tenacity, the hard work, and the genius of the Italian people have contributed to the progress of mankind.

The danger of all this and its disastrous consequences for Italy and for the Allied cause, were clearly recognized by the Consultative Committee, who at the end of December recommended to the Allied Governments the handing back to the Italian Government of the provinces administered by the Allied Military Government. As a result, the A.C.C. consented to reduce the activities of the Allied Military Government in the zone behind the front and on 11 February the Italian Government resumed control of the liberated provinces with the exception of Naples and the important area round that city, which remained under the Allied Military Government.

The law for the elimination of Fascism had been promulgated, and under a subsequent Order in Council a commission was set up to carry out its provisions, as it was out of the question to set up as many commissions as there were government offices. But it very soon became clear that this law provided only for the elimination of undesirable elements in state employ and in public bodies under state control. Meanwhile many private organizations which had supported Fascism and had thus enjoyed a privileged position and made enormous profits, remained entirely outside its scope. The order in Council, called the 'Expurgation Law', was therefore amended by Casati, the Lord Privy Seal, but these amendments were strongly opposed by several ministers. The tampering with some legal conceptions, sanctified by time, caused much perturbation. I had the proposals examined by such eminent jurists as Dr. De Nicola, Professor Forti, and Professor Altavilla, who suggested a series of alterations. But the final draft was only submitted to the succeeding Government.

The Order provided for the appointment of a High Commissioner, who, with the personnel whom he chose, was to carry out its provisions. The High Commissioner appointed was Tito Zaniboni who had been in prison and *confino* for so many years.

          ↣   ↣   ↣

About this time I received the reply from President Roosevelt to the letter which I had sent by General Donovan. Roosevelt thanked me for having written to him so frankly, 'like an old soldier', for this enabled him to answer with equal frankness. He fully appreciated the efforts I and my Government had made to stand shoulder-to-shoulder with the Allies and was ready to acknowledge our loyal co-operation. But in his opinion, only a democratic government based on the collaboration of all the anti-Fascist parties, would be able to obtain the maximum effort from the country for an even greater participation in the war. Roosevelt would examine the Italian situation again after such a government had come into existence.

At that moment Mr. Macmillan, who was very closely

associated with the British Prime Minister, returned from England where he had been. He expressed a desire to see me, so a meeting was arranged at which Mason-MacFarlane, Riber, Caccia, Prunas, and I were present. Macmillan said that Churchill was very friendly to me personally, but wished that as soon as possible I would set up a really democratic government. Macmillan insisted that we did not realize the importance of public opinion in England. There was great hostility to Italy because she had declared war on a nation traditionally friendly, when that nation was on the edge of the abyss. Furthermore, the English did not forget that the Mediterranean campaign had cost the Allies 200,000 dead.

The Government and the Press kept the English informed of all that my Government had done, but Macmillan said that as a people they were very slow to change their attitude.

This may seem a defect to you Italians [observed Macmillan], but it has its compensating quality which is that public opinion does not oscillate violently and when they think it right, they will once again become your faithful friends. Only a man like Churchill who is so beloved and respected, can afford the luxury of swimming against the current, as he did in his speech when he praised Italy. But powerful as he is, there are limits beyond which he cannot go, if he does not want to cause a serious reaction.

It was therefore essential for us to pay serious attention to this factor, and to continue to give our loyal co-operation as we had in the past, not to allow ourselves to be discouraged, and to await the future with patience.

CHAPTER XVI

The Constitutional Compromise

As I received unceasing requests from the Allies for the formation of a democratic government representative of all parties, I decided once again to approach their leaders so as to discuss the question of their co-operation. But I did not succeed, for every party made it a condition that the King should abdicate. I had a most interesting discussion on the question with Dr. De Nicola, an outstanding constitutional lawyer. With clear-cut logic he proved to me that the King represented nothing but an element of division among Italians, therefore it was essential to find a formula which was not abdication, to which he would agree and which would mean his disappearance from the scene. Dr. De Nicola told me that he had had many talks with Croce, Sforza, and other party leaders, and he had induced them to abandon their demand for the withdrawal of the Crown Prince; he promised to work out his plan in detail and come and see me again.

In the course of a few days he returned to Salerno and told me that he thought that the King should appoint the Crown Prince Lieutenant-General of the Kingdom, handing over to him permanently all the royal prerogatives, and that the King should retire into private life. De Nicola said that he had asked for an audience to place this proposal before the King. In view of his great knowledge I did not raise any objections, though it seemed to me to be merely begging the question. We had already had experience of a Lieutenant-General, but never of one with complete and permanent royal powers. In my ignorance of constitutional law I thought it would create an anomalous situation. We should have a King permanently deprived of all authority but with the empty title, and in his place a Lieutenant-General permanently in possession of all the royal powers, without the title of King.

If I had been in the King's place I should not have hesitated to choose abdication in the interest of the Crown Prince, who would have ascended the throne with far greater prestige. I had understood why the King would not abdicate on 25 July; he did not wish to leave his son to deal with such a complicated situation, but to handle it himself. But after his arrival at Brindisi, with the Malta armistice signed, with war declared on Germany and the situation more or less stabilized, the King could with advantage have withdrawn in favour of the Crown Prince.

De Nicola had a series of talks with the King, who very reluctantly accepted the plan in principle. The plan, which was to take effect when Rome was liberated, was communicated to me by the King so that I could inform General Mason-MacFarlane and the Allied Governments.

It had already been laid down, and I had told Mason-MacFarlane, that as soon as we reached Rome I would resign. The King would then have no difficulty in discussing with the party leaders who were in hiding in the city the formation of a democratic government. But I thought that to announce simultaneously the appointment of a Lieutenant-General and the formation of a new government would be neither logical nor prudent. It would mean two crises at the same time, one constitutional, and the other governmental, and I believed that as the King had agreed to the Lieutenant-Generalship it would be better to put it into effect at once. It did not now seem likely that we should be in Rome in the near future and the Crown Prince would have time to familiarize himself with his new functions before arriving in Rome. I explained my point of view to the Minister of the Royal

Household, and the King called a meeting of all the Ministers and read a declaration in which he stated his decision to nominate his son as Lieutenant-General, but this would only come into effect after and not before the liberation of Rome. It was obvious that the news, which was in the possession of so many people, could not be kept secret, and it immediately spread with many alterations and additions.

It seemed to me desirable to put a stop to all these inaccurate reports by publishing the complete text of the King's declaration. I spoke to De Nicola about it and he entirely agreed with me and promised to speak to the King. But a most unexpected Allied intervention took place.

General Mason-MacFarlane, Mr. Macmillan, and Mr. Murphy had an audience with the King to present the British Ambassador, Sir Noel Charles, who had just arrived in Naples from Brazil to act as British political representative and as a member of the Consultative Commission. When the presentation was over the Allied delegates immediately raised the question of the publication of the act of the appointment of the Lieutenant-General. The King was very much surprised, all the more so as it is not etiquette to raise any question with the King which has not been mentioned in the request for an audience. The King replied that he would consider the matter and communicate his decision.

At the moment I was in bed with very bad rheumatism, but Prunas came very late that evening to tell me what had occurred. The next morning I struggled up and went to Ravello to see the King. I found him very angry and promised him that I would do all in my power to postpone the transfer of powers until we reached Rome. He was rightly very insistent on this point and said: 'I left Rome

L

as King with Marshal Badoglio and I want to return as King with Marshal Badoglio.' The Allied delegates were waiting for me at the Villa Cimbrone, where there was immediately a very heated discussion on the question. The American, Mr. Murphy, took a specially strong line. I used every possible argument to convince them that the King's request did not alter the substance of his declaration, it only meant showing consideration and sympathy to a sovereign seventy-five years old, who, if he had committed faults, had the merit of having dismissed Mussolini, of having asked for an armistice, of having declared war on Germany, and of having fought loyally side by side with the Allies. I was sure that the Allies would agree to the proposal to publish the official statement with reference to the Lieutenant-General at once, but that the transfer of power should not take place until in their opinion the King could return to Rome.

I was convinced, and so was Prunas, that the Allied representatives had accepted my proposal, and on my return I told the King so in the presence of Prunas, and the King thanked me very warmly for what I had done.

The next morning I received a communication from an Allied source, which was being released to the Press at the same time. This stated that the King had announced his irrevocable decision to nominate his son as Lieutenant-General of the Realm, and that this would take effect, and the royal powers would be transferred, as soon as the Allied troops entered Rome. The formula which I had proposed, and which I thought had been accepted by the Allies, had been changed at the last moment.

The harsh way in which the King had been treated immediately produced considerable discontent among many sections of the people. The Allied representatives hastily announced in the Press and on the wireless, that they had limited themselves to advising the King. I talked to General Mason-MacFarlane about this; he told me that the King was very much annoyed by this interference of which he had had no warning, and that he had remarked that he had been put up with his back to a wall. I pointed out that the statement of the Allied delegates, that they had only given advice, was to say the least, disingenuous.

'If it was advice,' I added, 'it was given at the point of the pistol.'

      ∿   ∿   ∿

Meanwhile, as I have already related, Palmiro Togliatti, the head of the Communist Party, had arrived in Naples.

He at once made a speech which by its seriousness and objectivity, had a great effect on the people. Dealing with the existing situation he said that the Italian people must pursue two aims: the first was to give still more support to the armed forces in their fight against the Germans, the second was the intensification of the struggle to eliminate all Fascist elements. He expressed his readiness to co-operate with my Government and not to raise the question of the monarchy at the moment, but to leave it to the decision of the Constituent Assembly.

In another speech which he made at Potenza, Togliatti declared that Communism intended to respect the family and religion, and not to collectivize small properties. Communism wanted another economic system and an improvement in the condition of the working classes. He believed that everybody would support this programme, but a good many people did not believe in his sincerity.

Anyhow the declaration of Togliatti, that is to say of the Communist Party, caused a perfect ferment among the other parties as offering a chance of escape from the blind alley into which they had strayed.

In addition, the King's declaration about the Lieutenant-General seemed to remove all the obstacles which
up to the moment had prevented them from collaborating
with my Government, and several of their leaders got in
touch with me. I at once took the precaution of warning
the ministers in office; I told them that we should never
obtain better political conditions from the Allies unless
there were a reorganization of the Government. For the
good of the country and without a thought of themselves,
the ministers unanimously placed their resignations in
my hands.

I had first of all a talk with Croce, who assured me of
the support of the Liberal Party; Rodinò said the same
thing for the Christian Democrats. I knew that I could
count on the Socialists and the Communists, and I was
told that the Democratic Labour Party would also support
me. The only party which was hostile was the Action
Party, which said that I was not a fit person to be the head
of a government. But even if this party held aloof, five out
of the six were ready to collaborate, and therefore I should
be able to claim that the Government was the expression
of the popular will.

I immediately got over one difficulty by promising the
representatives of the various parties that they would all
join the Cabinet on a basis of equality. The chief obstacle
to rapid action was the assigning of the different ministries
to the different parties; they all put in claims to certain
posts and particularly that of the Minister of Internal
Affairs. In the end, by creating a representative of each
party a minister without portfolio, and by a system of
checks and balances in the various posts, I succeeded in
forming a Cabinet which was supported even by the
Action Party.

A great many people at once asked, Why are there so many ministers without portfolios? In the past it had been the custom to appoint as a minister without portfolio some outstanding personality whose name would strengthen the Government. For this reason I decided to appoint Benedetto Croce, whose name was known and honoured by everyone, and because at his age he could not have undertaken the hard work of a ministry. But Sforza also wanted to be a minister without portfolio; Rodinò immediately said that as he had been a minister several times and Sforza only once, he expected a similar honour. The Socialists and the Communists next demanded to have representatives among these super-ministers, and so Togliatti and Mancini were added.

Although this made the Cabinet rather top-heavy, there was an advantage in having a certain number of ministers who were not burdened with the heavy day-to-day work of a ministry, and who could therefore study particular problems. Every ministry in the new Cabinet had an under-secretary of a different political party from that of its minister.

At the first meeting of the ministers and under-secretaries the general lines of the political programme were laid down, the actual drafting being left to the ministers without portfolios. Then arose the thorny question of the oath on taking office; I proposed that before the ministers signed the oath, I should read the following declaration to the King:

Your Majesty, I have the honour to present the members of the new Government. They belong to every party, and while not abandoning their party allegiances, they are ready at this grave moment to subordinate these to the need for agreement, which is indispensable for the salvation of the country.

The formula was accepted and the swearing in was accomplished without any difficulty.[1]

[1] For the list of the members of the outgoing Cabinet see p. 123. By an Order in Council of 22 April 1944 the King appointed Marshal Pietro Badoglio Head of the Government. Senator Benedetto Croce, Count Sforza, Noble Giulio Rodinò di Miglione, Professor Pietro Mancini, Dr. Palmiro Togliatti, Ministers without Portfolio. Minister for Foreign Affairs, Marshal Badoglio. Minister for Internal Affairs, Dr. Salvatore Aldisio (a), Minister of Justice, Professor Vincenzo Arangio Ruiz (b). Minister of Finance, Signor Quinto Quintieri (c). Minister of War, General Taddeo Orlando. Minister of Marine, Admiral Raffaele de Courten. Air Minister, General Renato Sandalli. Minister of Education, Professor Adolfo Omodeo (d). Minister of Public Works, Signor Alberto Tarchiani (e). Minister of Agriculture and Forests, Dr. Fausto Gullo (f). Minister of Communications, Dr. Francesco Cerabona (g). Minister of Industry, Commerce and Labour, Dr. Attilio di Napoli, (h).

By Decrees dated 24 April 1944, the King, on the recommendation of the Head of the Government, appointed Dr. Renato Morelli Under-Secretary of State in the Cabinet Offices, and also on the recommendation of the Head of the Government with the concurrence of the respective ministers, appointed the following Secretaries of State: for Internal Affairs, Dr. Nicola Salerno and Dr. Filippo Caraccioli; for Justice, Dr. Nicola Lombardo; for Finance, Professor Antonio Presenti; for War, Dr. Mario Palermo; for Marine, Dr. Domenico Albergo; for Education, Dr. Angelo Raffaele Jervolino; for Public Works, Dr. Adolfo Cilento; for Agriculture and Forests, Professor Mario Bergami; for Posts and Telegraphs, Dr. Mario Fano. Railways and Road Transport, General Giovanni Di Raimondo; for Industry, Commerce, and Labour, Professor Francesco Sansonetti.

(a) Christian Democrat. (b) Liberal. (c) 'Banker'. (d) Action Party. (e) Action Party. (f) Communist. (g) Labour Democrat. (h) Socialist. (*Translator.*)

CHAPTER XVII

The Government of Democratic Unity

THE first meeting of the new Council of Ministers was held on 24 April 1944. I read the following statement on the foreign policy of the previous Government:

The Italian Government immediately set before itself one objective and a definite line of policy—to create between it and the Allied Nations an atmosphere of loyalty, confidence and collaboration. This was not easy after three years of bitter fighting.

The agony and the sufferings caused by the war still remained, as did also the open wounds caused by the cruel accusations in enemy propaganda. Everyone must recognize that the present state of affairs is entirely different from that of the days which preceded and followed the armistice. I think I may claim that the Allies now recognize the complete trustworthiness of the new Italy in its relations with them. This is the necessary starting-point of all future action, the *sine qua non* of all future initiative. The Allies know to-day beyond any possibility of doubt or contradiction, that all their victories are regarded by the Italian people as victories in a common cause.

Last March the U.S.S.R. welcomed our desire to restore Italo-Russian friendship, which should never have been destroyed, and to re-establish direct relations. This was a gesture of friendship which in those dark days profoundly touched the Italian nation. We follow with admiration the heroic struggle of the Russian people, the determination shown by its leaders, and the silent unity and strength with which the country is working in every sphere of national activity. We recognize the great political and military power of the Soviet in the councils of the nations and we wish once again to pursue a policy of friendship and mutual respect.

It must be remembered that we have been at war, or have

suspended diplomatic relations, with at least forty-four nations, and that therefore we have to renew these relations with about three-quarters of the world. The isolation created by the Fascist régime was total. Our immediate and most important aim has been to establish peace and friendship with each and all of the United Nations. We have already taken steps to re-establish our relations with the Republics of Latin America, to which we are especially bound by ties of culture, religion, and race. In those Republics there are millions of Italians who are regarded as well-disciplined, sober, and hard-working citizens. This effort will bear fruit in time.

We are not less anxious to begin as soon as possible the improvement and clarification of our relations with Greece and Yugoslavia. We wish to atone for the crimes committed against them by the former régime, and to build up friendship and good feeling with the nations on the other side of the Adriatic. The heroic conduct of the Garibaldi division, which recently has earned another citation by Marshal Tito, as well as of the detachments fighting with the Greek partisans, are the best augury for our success.

Last October I expressed publicly our feelings of friendship for France, after the unhappy disagreements of recent years. General de Gaulle has spoken in a way which shows his sympathy and belief in future friendly relations, a feeling which I entirely share. M. Massigli, the Ambassador, has been in frequent touch with us, and relations have been established between us and the French Committee of Liberation. The presence of French troops on the Italian front has created—as it was certain to do—a feeling of comradeship among our men, which is a further proof of the need for a *rapprochement* between our two countries—there is indeed—no ground for serious disagreement. I wished to give expression to this goodwill, so I sent a telegram to the Commander-in-Chief of the French forces, at the moment when they were disembarking in Italy.

And as I am speaking of comradeship in arms, I want to refer to the sympathy which immediately grew up between our troops serving with the 8th Army and the Polish Expeditionary

Force—the heroic representatives of a nation which, since the days of our Risorgimento and their first Risorgimento, has always had the closest ties of culture and ideals with Italy.

Without pretending to make an exhaustive survey at this meeting of the whole field of foreign affairs, I want to record that after the armistice, all the neutral countries—Argentine, Portugal, Spain, Sweden, Switzerland, and Turkey—continued to recognize the King's Government as the only legitimate one, notwithstanding the events which led to the creation under the protection of German bayonets, of the so-called Fascist Republican Government. I must call particular attention to the attitude and behaviour of Switzerland—to her generosity and help to the thousands of Italian refugees who found sanctuary on her territory from the persecution and terrorism of the Nazis and Fascists. This has added yet another tie, that of gratitude, to the friendship and common interests which have always existed between the two countries.

We also received sympathy and support from the Hungarian and the Roumanian peoples; despite pressure from Berlin on their respective Governments, they recognized the legitimate Italian Government and its accredited representatives until their countries were overrun by the Germans. It was with the deepest sorrow that we saw the events which followed the German *coup de main* and which have temporarily removed those countries from the comity of free nations.

I must add that at the beginning of last November the Government communicated to the Allies its decision to adhere to the Atlantic Charter, and last March to rejoin the International Labour Office. These two steps show very clearly our firm determination to take our place once again in the great international family of nations, with which Fascism had destroyed every tie and contact.

At the next meeting of the Council of Ministers on 27 April the Government outlined its programme in the following statement, which was immediately released to the Press and the wireless:

The programme of the present Government is the outcome of its origin and its membership. Formed by representatives of the anti-Fascist parties it is not a Government of parties at variance with each other, but a union of those parties for the good and honour of the country, whose sole object is to combine their forces so as to ensure the best possible solution of all the urgent and grave problems of the moment.

As a result, other problems, although their importance is recognized, are put on one side. The first of such questions is the future constitution of the State, which can only be decided when the country is freed and the war is won. The Italian people will then be called upon to elect a constituent assembly by universal suffrage. At the appropriate moment the Government will draft the necessary electoral law.

It is impossible to ignore the fact that two world wars have profoundly altered the economic and moral conditions of life and social relations. These call for radical reforms for which all parties, according to their views and programmes, are prepared; but these reforms, constitutional, political, administrative and economic, cannot be undertaken under war conditions, while Italy is divided into two parts, the larger portion being still occupied by the enemy.

Our first and greatest task is to carry on the war for the liberation of Italy from the foreign enemy in league with the remnants of the régime which for twenty-two years oppressed the country and finally brought about its ruin. In the struggle now being waged our soldiers are showing their legendary courage, which the former régime had not been able to inspire while forcing them to espouse a cause at variance with the whole history of the Italian people, and at the same time failing to provide them with the necessary weapons. With a new democratic government and freed from the feeling of frustration, our fighting men will be united and animated by the same spirit. Provided with ever-increasing supplies of munitions they will thus be able to increase their contribution to the Allied war effort. The Government will regard it as its duty to support by every means in its power the forces of our heroic patriots;

whatever party they represent they are all at one in the determination to free Italy and defeat the Germany of Hitler.

To the moral exigencies of war there is linked not only the severe punishment of all traitors, but also the elimination of all Fascist elements, which will convince all Italians that those who took a prominent part in the former régime are no longer able to work for the external and internal enemy. This desire for a feeling of security can only be satisfied by the removal from public life and the administration of all those who might be a danger to the State. This undertaking must not be inspired by a spirit of revenge, because all will wish to forgive and forget the past, to turn over a new page and re-establish confidence between Italians. It must be looked upon as a necessity for the salvation of the country, which must never again fall into the ways of life which led to horror and shame. This work has already been begun, and the Government will see that by just and energetic measures it will be carried to a successful conclusion as soon as possible.

Our chief aim is to give the population, and particularly those who have suffered most, conditions of life less hard than those of the last few months, which were brought about by destruction, by general impoverishment, by interrupted communications, and by lack of transport. It is essential to revive industry and agriculture; to promote the internal exchange of foodstuffs; to wage war against speculation; to obtain the necessary raw materials from abroad; to begin the reconstruction of public buildings, bridges, and roads; and at the same time to carry on the war.

For the accomplishment of such tasks the Government, recognizing the difficulties of the moment, counts on the active support of the professional organizations and of all categories of workers.

There remains finally the work of administration; this has already begun and must become more efficient, although the offices of the ministries are nothing but empty shells. They lack archives and personnel, the staffs are not only small in number but there are many gaps and inequalities. All these problems will be overcome, and as soon as practicable the Government means to re-establish taxation and state control of the finances. At the same time, working in collaboration with the Committees of Liberation, it will create as a symbol of the non-existent Parliament, a Consultative Council to which it will report at intervals on its activities.

This is the necessarily restricted programme to whose execution we shall devote all our energies, looking for the whole-hearted support of the nation without distinction of classes or parties, so that Italy may rise again.

As a matter of fact this programme did not represent any change from that of the previous Government.

There was, however, one novelty, the announcement of the Consultative Council to which the Government would report on past and future activities. There were no details as to how this would be constituted because this question had not been studied. The Ministers without Portfolios were charged with the drawing up of the constitution and working of this Council. I collected the documents relating to the analogous French body and sent them to Croce.

The meetings of the Council of Ministers were attended by seventeen ministers and the Under-Secretary of State in the Cabinet Office, Dr. Morelli. As he was my personal assistant I was well able to appreciate his intelligence and experience. In view of the polished verbosity of some of the ministers, and the lack of discipline of some of the others who interrupted the proceedings without addressing the chair, it was a difficult body to control. But little by little order was established and the work got on more quickly.

It was agreed to appoint Professor Omodeo as Head of the Commission for the elimination of Fascism, and Count Sforza as Head of the 'Purge Commission'. Tito Zaniboni was given charge of caring for the refugees. The 'Purge' law was carefully examined and Casati's draft was approved with some amendments.

I then gave a detailed review of the state of our armed forces, military, naval, and air. Togliatti intervened to assert that it was necessary to discuss the question of volunteers. I replied that I had already taken up the question with General Mason-MacFarlane, so as to find out if the Allied Governments would consent to the recruiting of volunteers and would provide them with arms and ammunition. The General had replied that the Allies would not permit the enrolment of volunteers. I explained to the ministers the state of the negotiations with regard to prisoners of war, which were extremely unsatisfactory.

In the end the new ministers were able to realize that the preceding Cabinet, although it had had such very limited means at its disposal, had not wasted its time.

꘎   ꘎   ꘎

The new Ministry was received with approval and sympathy. The foreign Press unanimously praised its composition and prophesied its success. The ending of party strife had an excellent effect in the country, and it was hoped that the divisions which had weakened our war effort were at an end.

Churchill, who had followed the internal politics of Italy with the greatest attention, showed his pleasure by returning three of our cruisers, and, as I have already said, by sending us five squadrons of aircraft.

I took the opportunity thus provided to discuss with the ministers our relations with the Allies. It was decided to set up a committee consisting of myself, Togliatti, Sforza, and Tarchiani to consider our future policy. I showed them my February letter to Roosevelt and his reply, and told them that I had written another letter to him, reminding

him of his promise to re-examine our political situation as
soon as a democratic government had been established.

I explained that it seemed to me the right moment to
invite Kirk, Charles, and Kostilev to come and see me, to
discuss the condition of the country and to ask for their
help to obtain an improvement in our status. I ended by
saying that I would tell the ambassadors that if the present
Government was not successful in obtaining the improvement it asked for, it would quickly lose all support in the
country and would be obliged to resign.

Sforza, who had originally offered to go to the United
States, finally abandoned this project, because if his mission
had failed, it would have been a setback for the Government. Not only did all the members of the committee
agree to my suggestion but Sforza said that he would do
his best to persuade Kirk to support our request, and
Togliatti undertook to do the same with Bogomolof and
Kostilev.

I asked Mr. Kirk to come and see me and explained to
him what we had done and how much more we should
have been able to do, if the Allies had helped us. The
Ambassador promised to lay our requests before his
Government, but as I had already written to Roosevelt
I did not go into the matter at any great length with Kirk.

On the other hand I was very much more explicit with
Charles, Bogomolof, and Kostilev. I pointed out to them
all the contradictions in the conduct of the Allies who,
while perpetually praising our willing collaboration, would
not agree to increasing our war potential. I gave them a
picture of the state of our finances, demonstrating that
though the Allies and we were engaged in studying the
means to prevent inflation, the financial burdens laid on
us and the exorbitant rate of exchange, produced directly
and immediately the very thing they wished to avoid. I

recalled the treatment of our prisoners and said that while Italian troops were fighting bravely beside the Allies in the front line, a few miles in the rear Italian prisoners were carrying out fatigue duties under the command of Allied officers. Finally I took up the question of the Allied Control Commission which, though it was supposed to be a help, was really a hindrance to all the work of the Italian Government.

Both Charles and Bogomolof asked me to send them an *aide mémoire* of what I had said and this I did at once. I heard afterwards that Charles had sent on his copy to his Government with a strong recommendation that it should be acted on.

◦   ◦   ◦

The Minister of Education, Professor Omodeo, was a man of great intelligence and culture, but lacking in judgement. He issued a decree suppressing the faculties instituted by his predecessor Cuomo at the University of Bari and at the Teachers' Training College set up by the province at Salerno, as well as another decree about a veterinary school at Naples.

There were demonstrations and a strike among the students, and the heads of the various institutions resigned; in fact, complete chaos reigned. It could not be denied that the Minister was right from the point of view of discipline and the proper conduct of the studies; on the other hand, it had to be remembered that given the situation and the difficulty of communications, the students were faced with the greatest difficulties in pursuing their courses. As a result of the opposition he had aroused, the Minister was obliged to give way, which naturally did not increase his prestige.

◦   ◦   ◦

There was a growing agitation among the state employees and the worst-paid workers for a revision of their
salaries and wages. An increase had been given by the
previous Government, but this proved to be insufficient.
The employers were agreed on the necessity for an increase
in wages and the Government was ready to do the same
for its employees, for it knew that a man with a family
could not live on the present rate of pay.

There were many meetings of experts with the Allied
Control Commission which was absolutely opposed to the
increases, and instead proposed to augment the ration. As
a matter of fact it was announced that the bread ration
of 200 grammes would be raised on 1 July to 300 grammes,
and as long as I was in the Government this was the only
concession which could be obtained. The Allies were
afraid that the raising of salaries and wages would produce more inflation. But they did not remove the other
causes of the drop in the value of money.

There was one other incident at this time which I
remember. Signor Ricciotti Garibaldi called on the Allied
authorities at Naples and said that he wished to see me.
I refused to receive him.

Shortly afterwards Ezio Garibaldi, a 'Consul General'
in the Fascist Militia and one of the leaders of the party,
reached our lines. His statements aroused so much suspicion in the minds of the officers of the British Intelligence Service, that they placed him in an internment
camp. Mason-MacFarlane came to tell me about this,
and we agreed that both the Garibaldis should be sent to
an island and closely guarded.

CHAPTER XVIII

The Liberation of Rome: The Lieutenant-Generalship: The New Government

GENERAL ALEXANDER had undoubtedly made a profound study of his military operations in Italy and had recognized the causes of his lack of success. Consequently he had radically changed his plans, concentrating all his available resources in one area. He left a thin covering force in the Adriatic sector which was obviously of secondary importance, and by a carefully co-ordinated and rapid manœuvre, had massed his two armies in front of the 'Gustav' line. He chose as the spearhead of the attack the French Corps, consisting chiefly of Moroccan troops, and the Polish Corps, both imbued with the spirit of the offensive. The British and the Americans were on either flank, the former to the south-west and the latter to the north-west of Cassino, and they would certainly be inspired to emulate the dash of the French and the Poles.

After a bitter resistance the Germans began to fall back, losing one strong position after another. Marshal Kesselring then made, in my opinion, the most serious mistake. Hoping perhaps to retrieve the situation, he threw all his remaining reserves into the battle. This meant that he had no forces at his disposal to cover the inevitable withdrawal, and only postponed for a few days the very rapid collapse of the 'Gustav' line. The Americans on the west established contact with the troops on the Anzio beachhead, who then went over to the attack.

I hastened to send my warmest congratulations to General Alexander, telling him at the same time of the ardent desire of the Italian Corps of Liberation to be sent

M

to the front as soon as possible. General Alexander welcomed this request, and said that he had always been very
pleased with the conduct of our detachments in the front
line, and that he had given orders for the army corps to
go into action at once. It began the attack in the mountain
sector and met with complete success.

The advance of the Allied troops became more rapid
and shortly afterwards we were informed that the advance
guard had entered Rome.[1]

General Mason-MacFarlane came to see me and asked
me to go with him to see the King at Ravello. On the
way he explained that, as the Allied troops had now
entered Rome, it was essential that the King should at
once sign the decree handing over the royal power and
prerogatives to the Lieutenant-General. He added that it
was impossible to grant the King's request that he should
go to Rome, he must sign the decree and retire, because
the American and British Press expected that the transfer
of powers would take place on the day that Rome was
liberated.

For reasons of security the Allied authorities could not
consent to the King going to Rome until the enemy was
compelled to retreat some distance from the city, which
would take some days. Such a delay in the signing of the
decree would antagonize public opinion in England and
the United States, and arouse doubts as to the validity of
the royal proclamation.

As soon as we arrived at Ravello General Mason-
MacFarlane explained all this to the King and asked him
to sign the decree, which in the meantime I had sent for
from Salerno. But the King declared that he would not
sign it unless he were given a letter signed by the Head of
the Government informing him officially that the Allies

[1] 4 June 1944. (*Translator.*)

refused to allow him to proceed to Rome immediately. With General Mason-MacFarlane's agreement I at once wrote and signed the letter, stating that notwithstanding the earnest and frequently expressed desire of the King to reach Rome by any means available, the Allied Supreme Command could not accede to this request, and therefore it was unavoidable that the decree should be signed at Ravello. His Majesty then appended his signature appointing his son Lieutenant-General of the Realm, conferring the royal prerogatives on him in perpetuity, and I countersigned.

So ended the reign of a King who, for forty-four years in good and evil fortune, had guided the destinies of Italy.

Now that the Lieutenant-General had taken up his office, I hurriedly consulted the experts in the Cabinet office as to whether, according to constitutional practice, the Cabinet should resign. The answer was that as the transfer of powers was irrevocable, the Cabinet should resign in order to leave the Lieutenant-General free either to confirm it in office or to choose new ministers. I called a meeting of the Cabinet and informed the members what had happened at Ravello, and of the advice I had received —that it was necessary for us to resign. Signor Arangio Ruiz, the Lord Privy Seal, speaking as a legal expert, maintained that this was not the case.

But the next day when I was going to Naples to see the Lieutenant-General and receive his instructions, General Mason-MacFarlane asked me to go to his office on my way to discuss some urgent and important questions. He told me that during the morning he had sent for Dr. De Nicola, who had given the same opinion as my experts in the Cabinet Office, that according to constitutional practice, the whole Cabinet must resign. General Mason-MacFarlane also said that it was not advisable to increase the Cabinet, which was already so large, by creating other ministries. It would therefore be better for me to go to Rome without a Cabinet, as in that way it would be possible for me to include in the new Government the politicians who were in Rome, leaving behind me the members of the resigning Cabinet.

I told him that I should have to return to Salerno and call a Cabinet meeting in order to tell the members what he had said, but Mason-MacFarlane objected that there was not time for that. As it was Tuesday he had only Wednesday to publish the news of the resignation of the Government and to arrange a meeting of the political leaders who were in Rome, for Thursday. He further said that I and six ministers, one for each political party, must leave by air for Rome on Thursday morning. This meeting had originally been fixed for Saturday, but now had to be held two days earlier. There was nothing for me to do but to go to the Lieutenant-General, who had already been coached by Mason-MacFarlane. He accepted the resignation of the Cabinet, and invited me to form a new Government to include the politicians in Rome. I got back to Salerno very late that evening and it was not till the following morning that I could inform the Cabinet of what had happened.

As laid down, I and the six ministers left by air for Rome on Thursday morning; at the Grand Hotel we found the leaders of the six parties and Signor Bonomi waiting for us. These leaders were: Casati, Liberal; Ruini, Democratic Labour; De Gasperi, Christian Democrat; Nenni, Socialist; Cianca, Action Party; the Communists were represented by Togliatti. I gave a brief account of the situation, Croce and Sforza adding a few words. I then begged the party leaders to discuss their future line of action among themselves, and to meet me again at the Grand Hotel at 6 p.m. to tell me what they had decided.

At 6 p.m. the proceedings began. Ruini stated that his party considered that if the Government was to be really and completely democratic, it must have a head who was not a soldier, and that this head should be Signor Bonomi. Similar declarations were made by Casati, De Gasperi, and Cianca without any comments. Nenni said that he was of the same opinion, and added that he did not approve of my having enlarged the Cabinet by appointing six ministers without portfolios; the new Government, in order to be able to act effectively and rapidly, should not consist of more than seven or eight ministers. I did not object to these observations as every one has a right to his own opinion. But the Ministry which was set up later had five or six ministers without portfolios, a new Ministry, that of the Treasury, and an increased number of under-secretaries.

None of the ministers who had come with me had anything to add except Togliatti, who said that the Communists wished to act with the other parties, and therefore supported Ruini's motion, although he would regret being separated from me, as we had worked together so harmoniously.

I got up and shook Togliatti's hand, saying:

I must thank you and the leaders of the other parties, who have expressed their views so clearly. I have served my country to the best of my ability, and I willingly resign my post into the more expert hands of my friend Bonomi, assuring him and all of you that I shall not limit myself to the simple act of resignation, but shall hold myself at your disposal for any information which you may desire. Let me add one thing. It is not because of any action on your part that you have met round this table in Rome; you were in hiding or living safely with friars in convents. The man who has done the work, who has shouldered the heaviest responsibilities, is that soldier, who as Ruini has said, does not belong to any party.

I then went to see the Lieutenant-General, who had arrived in Rome during the day, and told him what had happened, suggesting that he should at once send for Bonomi.

The next day I returned to Salerno.

On Monday I was told that General Mason-MacFarlane wanted to see me and Bonomi at the government offices at 2 p.m. He informed us that the new Government could not take office without the approval of the Allied Powers; as the three Governments—American, British, and Soviet —must consider this matter, some days would elapse before the necessary approval was received. He handed Bonomi the draft of a communiqué for the Press embodying this statement.

Bonomi was very much upset by this brusque and unexpected interference. I intervened, pointing out to Mason-MacFarlane that such a communiqué would deprive the Government of all authority before it even took office, and I thought it better not to issue any statement, but to wait a few days. In case there was a delay in receiving the *placet*, then a colourless message, which would as far as possible conceal the real state of affairs, could be issued to the Press.

Mason-MacFarlane accepted my suggestion and left. Bonomi questioned me about the formation of my two Ministries at Brindisi and Salerno, and whether the Allies had made a similar request. I replied that such a restriction had never been imposed on me; Mason-MacFarlane had simply noted the communication informing him of the composition of the new Cabinets.

As the ministers were coming and going in the government offices awaiting instructions, Bonomi called them into his room and told them of the decision of the Allied Governments. Naturally, that evening the news was all over Salerno and Naples, so in any case, the publication of the communiqué would have been superfluous.

This produced a crop of rumours, some of which were ridiculous. But one caused me serious anxiety; this was that the Allies, who for nine months had worked with me and my Government, showing us the most complete confidence, had made it a condition that I should be a member of the new Cabinet. To minimize the effect of such a deplorable situation, I went to see Bonomi, whom I found with Casati and Visconti-Venosta. I told Bonomi, who had been a friend of mine for over twenty years, that in order to save him trouble, if the Allies made such a condition, I was ready to work under him as Minister of Foreign Affairs or in any other post in which I could serve my country. But this was only in case of Allied intervention. Fortunately their intervention did not take the form I feared.

It was usual for the Head of the Government, on taking office, to make a declaration that he would undertake the same obligations towards the Allies as those of the previous Government. During my period of office the Allies were content with my signature to the appropriate document. They now asked for the signature not only of the Head of the Government, but of each of the ministers. This could hardly be regarded as a mark of confidence.

The unexpected change of Government caused much discussion and many recriminations.

The ministers of the previous and the new Government both accused Mason-MacFarlane and me of having acted too hastily. Others thought that it was a great mistake not to have asked the heads of the political parties in Rome to come to Salerno so as to explain the situation to them. Others were of opinion that it would have been better for me to have gone to Rome with the Government then in office and only later on to have begun negotiations with the political parties.

As all this was based on 'if's' and 'but's', there was no end to the arguments.

For me there was only one thing that mattered, and that needed no discussion; I could now enjoy with a clear conscience the rest of which I stood so badly in need.

❧ ❧ ❧

As soon as I resigned I sent the following telegrams to the heads of the Allied Governments:

To MR. CHURCHILL:

I am most grateful for the valuable support which you have given me during these nine months of hard work. I shall remember the generous and kind things which you have said about the Italian people on several occasions, as one of the clearest proofs that the labours of myself and my Government were not in vain. I trust that you will give my friend Signor Bonomi and his Government the support which has been an inspiration and a stimulus to me.

To PRESIDENT ROOSEVELT:

I wish to thank you for the support and help which you have given to the Italian people during particularly hard and difficult times. My resignation will not interrupt for a single day my efforts to promote friendship between Italy and the United

States. The remembrance of your friendship will be one of the happiest recollections of my public life.

To MARSHAL STALIN:

In resigning office I wish to thank you particularly for the proofs of friendship you have given to the Italian people and to me during sad and difficult days. These proofs of friendship will not be forgotten and are the best auguries for the continuing and loyal collaboration between our two peoples.

Among the replies that I received, the warmest was that of Mr. Churchill who wrote:

The work which you have done for the Italian people and for the cause of the United Nations during the last nine months has aroused general admiration. I am glad to know that the support I was able to give you was a help. Thank you very much for your message.

◦   ◦   ◦

As I end this brief account of those nine months, my heart goes out with gratitude to all those who served with me from 25 July, who shared the anxieties and hopes of that long period of suffering, and who upheld me by their devotion and their unwearied and conscientious work.

CHAPTER XIX

Italy and the Allies

To express a calm and impartial judgement on the relations between Italy and the Allies is extremely difficult. Difficult for an Italian whose love for his unfortunate country threatens to distort the objectiveness of his summing up: difficult for a citizen of one of the Allied countries and especially for an Englishman, who may be blinded by bitter feeling. I shall try to make this examination as impartial as I can.

I shall begin by admitting frankly, without any equivocation, all the grave faults we have committed. Italy declared war on 10 June 1940 when the situation of England and France was almost desperate. Mussolini asked for the honour of sending our aeroplanes to bomb London. From 10 June 1940 to 8 September 1943 the armed forces of Italy did their duty in fighting against the Allies. As I have already said, the representatives of Great Britain and America several times reminded me that they had lost 200,000 dead during the Mediterranean campaign.

I want to emphasize this, because so many Italians, by declaring that the Italian people did not want war, think that they have exonerated Italy. It is true that the Italian people did not want war, but they were compelled to fight. This is true of all wars, especially offensive wars; the people are hardly ever willing participants. It is an active and determined minority which forces a nation into war.

But I repeat, Italy fought for three years against the Allies, and it is only natural that the Allies should not forget this when, having asked for an armistice, we became co-belligerents. I therefore recognize the justice of

Churchill's phrase that Italy had to work her passage before she could become one of the United Nations.

    ⟶   ⟶   ⟶

But admitting the wrong we committed before 8 September 1943, we must consider the conduct of Italy and the Allies from that date up to the capture of Rome—that is to say, the period during which I was Head of the Government.

In my daily contacts with General Mason-MacFarlane, and for a brief period with General Joyce, I never made a promise which was not faithfully fulfilled. And in my relations with the respective chiefs of the Allied Governments, any obligation laid on my country was honoured. Roosevelt and more especially Churchill were unsparing in their approval. I can therefore confidently claim that during my period of office, Italy carried out all the terms of the armistice.

    ⟶   ⟶   ⟶

There was, it is true, one dark cloud over our relations, that was when I accepted the proposal of Moscow for an exchange of representatives, which compelled America and Great Britain also to send representatives. In Chapter XIV I have explained the facts of the case, which were:

1. I kept General Joyce and General Mason-MacFarlane entirely *au courant* with the negotiations.
2. Having signed an armistice with America, Great Britain, and Russia, I could not treat the U.S.S.R. differently from the other two.
3. That if Great Britain and the United States wished to remonstrate, they should have done so to the Russian representative and not to me.

    ⟶   ⟶   ⟶

In considering the conduct of the Allies, I must point out the obvious contradiction between the declarations of the British and American Governments and the behaviour of the Allied Supreme Command in the Mediterranean, held successively by Generals Eisenhower, Wilson, and Alexander.

As I have said, in the Quebec document and in all the communications from Roosevelt and Churchill, Italy was incessantly urged to take a more active part in the war against the Germans. We tried in every way to fulfil this request; it was our heart-felt desire, inspired not so much by the written statements of the Allies that the improvement in our lot would depend on our contribution to the war effort, as by our own pride. We did not wish the Allies to free our country without our help.

The proof of this is to be found not only in the preceding chapters but in the documents in the Appendix, which show not only the efforts I made to achieve this object, but also the limitations imposed by the Allied military command and the obstacles placed in our way. Were the Allies still obsessed by distrust of my country? But we had given indisputable proofs of our sincerity. Our feelings were shown unmistakably by men, women, and children when they attacked the German tanks with bottles of petrol in the streets of Naples.

When I attended the first meeting of the Consultative Council for Italy, I said to Vishinsky:

I declare that an enormous majority of the Italians are entirely hostile to the Germans and friendly to the Allies. If you doubt this, motor along the road from Naples to Avellino. The dumps of petrol and munitions are so high that you seem to be driving along a corridor. The pickets are sixty miles apart, and yet the dumps have never been attacked, which shows the feelings of the people towards the Allies.

In the first Allied attack at Montelungo a small Italian contingent took part, and fought bravely though they did not attain their objective. Therefore this distrust should not have existed, or if it did, it should have disappeared.

But not content with the obstruction of our military collaboration, the Allied Control Commission intervened to paralyse our efforts to restore order and discipline in the disorganized life of the country. Mr. Morrison, a member of the British Cabinet, wrote later: 'Care must be taken that the control encourages initiative, and does not stifle it.' But that stifling was exactly what happened. I cannot refrain from mentioning this, because it seriously retarded the work of restoring normal conditions in my country, and therefore still further weakened the efforts of Italy in the war of liberation.

The requisitioning by the Allies of private houses, of public buildings, and of industrial plants was carried out in haste, without any regard for the people who lived in the houses, and, even more important, without any regard for the common war effort.

In spite of orders from the Allied Supreme Command, irreparable damage was done by the Allied troops to palaces and historic buildings of great artistic value and also to their priceless contents; to the Royal Palaces at Naples and Caserta, and to the Academy of Fine Arts at Naples, to mention only the outstanding examples. The Government tried hastily to repair them and proposed the setting up of an Allied-Italian Committee to prevent such things happening in the future, but the suggestion was not even considered.

The Italian Government incessantly asked that the railway stations, post offices, telegraph, and telephone offices should be evacuated by the Allied troops, but our requests were rarely granted. A typical case of obstruction was that of the exclusive use by the Allies of the telegraph lines, Palermo–Naples and Palermo–Cagliari, which carried one Morse circuit. If they had been handed over to us we could have immediately adapted them to carry four circuits, giving two to the Allies and using the other two ourselves.

The lack of postal and telegraph facilities retarded the restoration of the economic life of the country.

The facilities on the railways, after the Government and the railwaymen had done all in their power to restore and repair them, might have been very much improved for the good of the general public. But the method of control by an Allied Committee in Naples was so slow and complicated as to paralyse all civilian traffic. In vain the Government asked again and again that the control of the railways should be handed back to it, undertaking to satisfy all the requirements of the Allied Military Command.

The same difficulties hampered road transport, owing to the often arbitrary requisitioning of lorries, motor-cars, and buses.

We asked vainly for the re-establishment of communications with Sicily and Sardinia, and for permission to use our own small ships of under 1,500 tons for coastwise traffic.

We also suffered considerably by the requisitioning for the exclusive use of the troops of entire industrial establishments (factories, mills, cement works, brick kilns, &c.) while machinery was removed and raw materials were damaged.

·◌·   ·◌·   ·◌·

According to a clause in the armistice of 29 September, Italy was obliged to furnish the Allied nations with all the Italian currency demanded and the Italian Government had to reimburse the Allied Governments for the cost of the occupation. The Allies derived great benefit from this clause, which was a serious obstacle to Italian economic recovery and to participation in the war.

·◌·   ·◌·   ·◌·

Finally I ask: Which would have contributed more to victory over the Germans, an Italy which remained inert and passive, or an Italy which, with Allied help, took a decisive part in the struggle?

The answer cannot be in doubt and the Allied leaders knew it, for they were incessantly inciting the Italian people to play their part, to strike hard and to give no quarter to the common enemy.

That is the reasonable and logical answer.

But what happened bore no relation to this premiss: instead of helping us, the Allies did all in their power to lower morale, to discourage enthusiasm, and to cramp our efforts.

Evidently reason did not hold sway.

·◌·   ·◌·   ·◌·

In order to understand this strange situation, it is necessary to abandon the sphere of pure reason and to wander into the complicated by-ways of international politics.

Both the United States and Great Britain declared that

Italy must resume her place among the free and democratic nations.

M. Vishinsky, in the name of the Soviet Government, explicitly declared that Italy must as soon as possible become free and great.

But did not these unanimous declarations on our future perhaps conceal substantial differences of points of view and of rivalry between the three great Allied states?

VAE VICTIS!

APPENDIXES

NOTE

In Parts I and II of this book I have tried to give the reader a complete, if very brief, account of the catastrophic position of Italy under the Fascist régime, and of the efforts that I made to return to a democratic form of government and to retrieve the past. In order to do this I limited my story to the essential facts.

In these appendixes I have collected some documents dealing with important questions which I did not wish to discuss at length in the preceding chapters as they would have interrupted my narrative of events.

The documents were compiled on my orders by the appropriate military and civil authorities.

DOCUMENT No. I

The Royal Italian Army

I. WHAT IT ACHIEVED

The state of the Army in the liberated provinces of the mainland and in the Islands immediately after the armistice, was as follows:

9 Mobile divisions.
12 Divisions for coastal defence.
Some small motorized units.
Territorial organizations and services, efficient in the Puglie, seriously disorganized in Calabria, non-existent in Sicily and in Campania.

The above forces amounted to 430,000 men, of whom half were in Sardinia. They possessed limited means of transport and were not equipped or armed for modern warfare. In spite of this they immediately attacked the Germans and continued to fight beside the Allies until 20 September 1943, on which date the Allied Military Mission issued instructions that Italian troops were not to participate in the fighting on Italian territory until further orders.

Later, as the result of repeated and urgent requests from the Government, permission was given to send a motorized unit of one infantry regiment and several batteries of artillery (2,500 men) to the front. This unit took up its position in the front line at the beginning of December 1943, on the flank of the American 5th Army. The courage and fighting spirit of the Italian troops were praised in a message sent by General Clark, commanding the American 5th Army, on 20 December 1943 to the Italian Command:

'I desire to congratulate the officers and men under your command on the success of their attack last night on Montel-lungo and in sector 343. This action shows the determination of the Italian soldiers to liberate their country from German control. Fighting in a hard and difficult terrain, the resolu-tion of the Italians to free their country's soil from the Nazi slavery, will serve as an example for all the European peoples who are fighting against German oppression.'

In spite of this message, all the requests of the Italian Government for its forces to take a larger share in the fighting were seldom acceded to. In fact, the Allied Control Commis-sion decided that the Italian troops in the front line were not to exceed 14,000 men. This limitation of numbers was always very strictly enforced by the Allied authorities despite Italian demands that it should be increased.

Owing to the need for reliefs the Italian Corps of Liberation consisted of 21,000 men—14,000 in the 7th contingent and 7,000 parachutists of the Nembo Division. They took an active share in the offensive which led to the liberation of Rome, but not to the extent that the Italian people desired, or which had been promised by General Eisenhower in the autumn of 1943. *This Corps was armed and equipped entirely with Italian matériel.*

The Allied Control Commission requested the Italian Government also to furnish:

101,000 men for purposes of internal security.
180,000 men to be employed by the Allies in various services.
45,170 men for the rear areas, Territorial units and services.

The greater number of these men were dispatched in a very short time.

There were Italian engineer and pioneer units who worked with the Allies in the forward areas. All these troops rendered important services immediately behind the front line, including the beach head at Anzio, and suffered their share of casualties. If these troops had been regarded as combatants, on the same system of classification as that used by the Allied Command for their own first- and second-line troops, the effective force of the Italian contingents would be more than double the number in the Italian Corps of Liberation. There were also 16,000 men serving in the anti-aircraft batteries.

The Italian troops in the Balkans attacked the Germans immediately after the publication of the armistice and later retired into the mountains. For many weeks the Germans were fighting against the nine Italian mobile divisions scattered over a wide tract of country, without contact with each other or the Italian Government. In addition, many small groups held out in isolated sectors. They were entirely cut off and received no help from the Allies. Later the Italian Government was authorized to re-establish communications with these troops, but although regular contact was maintained with the Garibaldi Division which was fighting with Marshal Tito, there was great difficulty with regard to the smaller and scattered units in the Balkans.

Only information received from the most reliable sources is included in the following description of the activities of the forces in the Balkan theatre. They represent but a fraction of the whole story:

1. A large part of the Pinerolo Division, of the Lancieri d'Aosta and elements of the Casali and Forlì Divisions, who

retired into the mountains of Thessaly in Greece, were engaged in active operations against the Germans until 14 October 1943, when their arms were forcibly seized by the Communist organization in spite of the protests of the British Military Mission. The Manfredini Alpine contingent of 2,000 men continued to fight in the Epirus Mountains.

2. In Albania the remnants of the Florentine and Brenner Divisions and some smaller units engaged the enemy in the mountains, where our men were joined by Albanian patriots.

3. The most important engagements in the Balkans in which Italian troops took part were in Yugoslavia. In December 1943, after several actions in which our troops fought single-handed or co-operated with Tito's partisans, the Garibaldi Division was formed exclusively of Italian units, and served with Tito's army. The Garibaldi Division fought in Montenegro and repulsed the sixth German offensive. There were many engagements with the Germans and the Chetniks, among the most important being those at Priepolij, Plevia, Jabuka, Kamena, Cora, Odaso, Broadarevo, Berena, Murina, and Andrevica. On several occasions Marshal Tito's communiqués made special mention of the Garibaldi Division.

4. In addition to this Division, smaller units, among them the Matteotti battalion, joined groups of the Partisans. According to an interview which Tito gave to a Reuter correspondent in May 1940, more than 80,000 Italians were fighting in Yugoslavia. Italian losses on this front were very heavy.

The courage and determination shown by the Italian troops in Yugoslavia frequently received official recognition both from the Allied military authorities and from Marshal Tito. Almost every day after 8 September 1943, the Allied wireless bulletins gave official and laudatory accounts of the work of the Italians in the Balkans. For example:

1. 3 January 1944. B.B.C. from London. 'The Yugoslav wireless states that during the fighting in the Novi Bazar sector the Italian units incorporated in the Army of Liberation have shown the greatest courage. The 3rd Brigade of the Garibaldi Division is worthy of special mention.'

2. 9 January 1944. Moscow Radio. 'In Yugoslavia in the Plevlya zone Italian troops during the last few days have wiped out several hundred Germans and captured a great quantity of booty.'

3. 23 March 1944. B.B.C. from London. 'According to information received from a German source, Italian units have launched a violent attack against the German positions in Bosnia, 70 miles east of Sarajevo. The battle continues.'

4. 24 March 1944. B.B.C. from London. 'To-day's communiqué from the Headquarters of the Army of Liberation in Yugoslavia states that an entire Italian division, plus several smaller units, is fighting with the Yugoslav army.'

5. 22 April 1944. 'Marshal Tito has sent a message of congratulation and thanks to the Italian Garibaldi Division for their heroic struggle against the Germans.'

6. 8 May 1944. B.B.C. from London. 'The Chief of Marshal Tito's Military Mission, General Wellebit, who is now in London, has declared that the Italian Garibaldi Division is extremely well disciplined, and a first-class fighting formation.'

2. WHAT THE ITALIAN ARMY MIGHT HAVE ACHIEVED

The Italian troops who were in various parts of the Puglie at the date of the armistice immediately joined the Allied troops in the common struggle to drive the Germans from Italian soil. During the first days the Allied Command invited and welcomed the help of the Italian forces. But on 21 September General Mason-MacFarlane, Head of the Allied Military Mission to the Italian Government, conveyed verbal instructions from the Allied Supreme Command, that the Italian troops were not to take part in the fighting until further orders. The Government immediately protested against this decision and on 22 September telegraphed to the Allied Commander-in-Chief declaring that the Italian troops wished to continue the fight against the Germans. No reply was received to this telegram.

On 29 September, at Malta, the Head of the Government spontaneously offered to use all the armed forces and the entire resources of the country on the side of the Allies in the struggle against the Germans; he specially mentioned the Nembo Parachute Division, and the two divisions of infantry which were in Sardinia. But this offer, as is clearly shown in the records of the Conference, was refused by General Alexander. He stated that 'the plans for the Italian campaign had already been most carefully worked out in all details, and in consequence, the participation of Italian troops could not be considered'. General Eisenhower said, 'I am sure that General Alexander could deal with the matter in such a way as to organize effective collaboration. I do not see any difficulty in allowing the Italian troops to enter Rome with the first troops to reach the city.' Despite General Eisenhower's words, *Italian participation in the struggle against the Germans was limited to the minimum, not by our fault and notwithstanding our continuous and repeated offers.*

On 30 September, the day after the Conference, a promemoria, which the Italian authorities had not been able to present at Malta, was sent to General Eisenhower and his Chief of Staff. It contained the following proposals for military collaboration: the utilization in the immediate future of seven Italian divisions and a motorized corps of about 10,000 men, another three divisions to follow in the near future, all to be equipped and armed from Italian supplies. The Allies were only asked to provide the means of transport to Italy for the troops in Sardinia and Corsica, and to authorize the use of Italian *matériel* in Sicily and Calabria. No direct reply was ever received.

On 3 October 1943, an offer was sent to the Head of the Allied Military Mission of the services of prisoners of war to form large active service units. This offer was repeated on 11 October and 26 October by the Italian High Command and subsequently on innumerable occasions, but always without success.

A few days after 8 October 1943, the Head of the Government had an interview with General Alexander, who declared himself to be in favour, in principle, of an effective participa-

tion by Italian troops in military operations. No action, however, was taken by the Allied authorities to implement this
declaration.

On 10 October 1943, the Italian High Command proffered
the services of the 1st Battalion of the Arditi[1] who were
specially trained in sabotage; the Allies were merely asked to
provide transport. This offer was refused.

On 12 October, at the time of the formal declaration of war
against Germany, Marshal Badoglio sent another letter to
General Eisenhower in the following terms:

'Now that Italy has declared war on Germany, if this is to be
more than a platonic gesture, it is essential that you should
accede to my requests, so that we may be able to co-operate as
fully as possible with the forces under your command. You
wrote to me that the eventual improvement of the armistice
terms will depend on the conduct of the Italian Government.
But without your help we shall be restricted to expressions of
good intentions.'

The Marshal then made the following offers:

1. Alpine troops, who will be extremely valuable in view of
   the mountainous nature of the terrain, and Grenadiers[2]
   amounting to four divisions. Transport to be provided by
   the Allies who have requisitioned all our ships.
2. We could furnish other divisions if our arms and equipment from Sicily and Tunisia were returned to us.
3. It would be possible to organize large formations of
   prisoners of war and volunteers desirous of fighting for
   Italy.

The Marshal wrote again two days later, 13 October, to
General Eisenhower; 'If you will help me in the ways which I
suggested in my letter of a few days ago, you will see our
forces multiply and they will be of the greatest service to our
common cause.'

However, on 17 October, General Taylor informed the
Italian Government:

[1] Italian 'Shock' troops. (*Translator.*)
[2] Regiments of the Royal Brigade of Guards. (*Translator.*)

'For the moment we do not intend to use any Italian troops for military operations except the motorized contingent. We propose to employ ten Italian divisions for the defence of the lines of communication in the peninsula and the Islands, some anti-aircraft batteries, and some engineer units. The Italian Air Force will be used exclusively in the Balkan theatre.'

This reply was very discouraging. The Head of the Government, however, assured the Allied Command of our full collaboration within the limits laid down, and reiterated our wish to give greater help, insisting again that there were four fully equipped divisions in Sardinia which could be used against the enemy.

On 22 October 1943, the Italian High Command pointed out to General Eisenhower, through the Italian Military Mission, that our Alpine regiments, specially trained for mountain warfare, were available and more suitable for use in broken and mountainous terrains than motorized troops.

On 26 October 1943, the Italian High Command instructed the Military Mission in Algiers to offer to transfer to the Allied authorities three divisions of infantry, one division of parachutists, three coastal defence divisions, one Alpine contingent, one Grenadier contingent, and other smaller units. The troops could have been used in the campaign against the Germans. Once again the offer was refused.

On 30 October General Eisenhower authorized the training of one Italian division for service in the front line. This training was begun immediately by the Italian High Command, who informed the Allies that the Legnano Division had been chosen. The training of this division was almost completed, the arms and equipment being entirely Italian. By a series of oral and written communications every obstacle was put in the way of the use of this division by the Allied military authorities; they also commandeered so much of the equipment that in the end the Legnano Division could not be used. Later General Alexander stated that Italian participation must be limited to the motorized contingent which was ready to go into action, and to a contingent of Alpine troops. The Italian Government once again pointed out that General Eisenhower had authorized participation on a very much larger scale.

On 28 October General Eisenhower replied to Marshal Badoglio's letter of 12 October in the following terms:

'I welcome with much pleasure the possibilities which you have pointed out.

'Temporary limitations make it impossible for the moment to accept some of your proposals which otherwise would be very welcome. . . .

'During the advance in northern Italy the need for mountain troops will become more acute. The quality of Italian Alpine troops is well known and we hope to avail ourselves of their help when the moment comes. . . .

'The occupation of Rome will no doubt necessitate the use of Italian troops.'

On 29 November 1943, the new Chief of the General Staff, Marshal Messe, in explaining his programme to the Allied Military Mission, pointed out the great value of the Italian Army and its need of personnel and equipment. No direct answer to his proposals was received.

On 1 January 1944, the Italian High Command insisted again that the Nembo Parachute Division should be used with the units which had gone into the front line a few days previously. It was only at the end of May that the Nembo Division was transferred from Sardinia to the Italian mainland. It was assigned to the Italian Corps of Liberation solely to provide reliefs for the troops in the front line, so that the Corps of Liberation was never allowed to exceed 14,000 combatant troops, as laid down in the order of the Allied Control Commission of 6 April 1944.

After these incessant refusals the Italian Government realized that, while the Allied Governments insisted on the need for greater Italian participation in the war, the Allied military authorities were entirely opposed to the effective collaboration of the Italian armed forces in military operations.

The Italian Army did not receive any help in arms and *matériel* for training combatant units, but in many cases

Italian arms which had been collected with the greatest difficulty for the use of our formations, *were seized by the Allied military authorities and sent to Yugoslavia and other countries*. The Allies requisitioned great quantities of *matériel*, arms and munitions, including:

> 360, 81-calibre mortars, and others of smaller calibre.
> More than two million rounds of small-arms ammunition.
> Many parts for under-water arms.

The particulars given in the preceding pages represent only the minimum of the repeated offers made by the Italian Government to the Allied military authorities and refused by them. All this serves to show that the Italian people 'did not seek a spurious rehabilitation by the exertion of others, but wished to regenerate Italy internally and internationally by their own courageous efforts'.

DOCUMENT No. II

The Royal Italian Navy

I. WHAT IT HAS DONE

THE important contribution of the Italian Navy to the war against the common enemy has so often been recognized by the Allied authorities that it seems almost superfluous to give a detailed account of its activities in this memorandum. It is sufficient to recall the speeches of Mr. Churchill on 22 February 1944 and 24 May 1944, and the statement of Admiral Cunningham, the Allied Commander-in-Chief in the Mediterranean zone, of 28 May 1944. I will therefore limit myself to a summary of the essential facts.

After the events which succeeded the publication of the armistice, the Italian naval forces consisted of:

> 5 battleships.
> 9 cruisers.
> 11 destroyers.
> 37 submarines.

40 torpedo-boats and corvettes.

30 motor torpedo-boats ('MAS').

Auxiliary vessels.

Of these ships some (battleships and cruisers) had been transferred according to the terms of the armistice to Allied bases, others to Italian ports in Liberated Italy such as Taranto, Brindisi, La Maddalena, and other ports which were defended by Italian troops against German attacks. In addition, the Italian Navy was in control of the important naval arsenal of Taranto and possessed efficient dockyards and services in southern Italy and Sardinia.

During the period 8 September 1943 to 30 April 1944, the Italian Navy carried out the following duties for the Allies:

1. 356 operational cruises, employing 432 ships, which steamed a total of 130,021 miles.

2. 542 non-operational movements, with a total of 219,168 miles.

3. 108 ships have been engaged in transporting 219,168 Italian troops and *matériel*, 114,512 miles.

4. 36 ships, cruisers and destroyers, acted as fast transports for 13,607 Allied troops, steaming 23,444 miles.

5. Provided escorts for 65 Italian steamships, steaming 21,009 miles.

6. The most important work done for the Allies was the escorting of 308 Allied convoys of a total of 4,032 ships of a total tonnage of 32,595,000. For this purpose 862 escorts were provided and they steamed 214,318 miles.

The total movements of ships in the Italian Navy from 8 September 1943 to 30 April 1944 amounted to 1,889 and covered a total of 646,370 miles. The following operations were carried out:

1. Bombardments of the Adriatic coast.

2. Patrol activity throughout the Adriatic to intercept enemy shipping and protect landings in Dalmatia.

3. Transport of Allied personnel from Albania and Greece.

4. Numerous missions by submarines and M.T.B.'s for the

transport to many localities of Italian and Allied saboteurs and agents. Several ships were lost in the course of these operations.

5. Supplies carried by submarines and destroyers for the troops in the Aegean Islands.

6. Sweeps by destroyers and torpedo-boats to intercept German naval forces, and for the protection of Italian positions in the Ionian Islands, Sardinia, and Corsica. Several ships were lost.

During the period 8 September 1943 to 30 April 1944, the losses of the Italian Navy were as follows:

1 battleship, 30,000 tons (*Roma*).
4 destroyers.
5 torpedo-boats.
1 corvette.
3 auxiliary cruisers.
1 submarine.
14 M.T.B.'s.

During the same period the casualties were as follows:

733 killed.
6,369 missing.
748 wounded.

The percentage of losses in relation to the total personnel engaged, was 20 per cent.

Although the figures for the total movements of the Allied fleets in the Mediterranean are not yet known, it can be confidently stated that the operations of the Italian Navy represent a high proportion of the total. This naturally enabled the Allies to transfer a large number of their ships to other theatres of war.

The activities of the Italian Navy outside the Mediterranean have also been important, as Mr. Churchill pointed out in his speech of 24 May 1944. Fast cruisers, based on Freetown, intercepted German commerce raiders in the Atlantic. A flotilla of submarines was at Bermuda, another with auxiliary vessels at Colombo.

Between 8 September 1943 and 31 March 1944, the Italian naval yards carried out 350 repairs to 130 Allied ships of a total tonnage of 900,000, representing 120,000 working days. More than 1,000 skilled mechanics were engaged in these repairs.

2. WHAT THE NAVY COULD HAVE DONE

Although the figures given above are very striking, the Italian Navy could have made an even greater contribution, if it had been allowed to do so by the Allies.

The two newest battleships were interned in an Egyptian port, with reduced crews and with the breech-blocks of their guns removed. These were the *Vittorio Veneto*, which was ready for sea, and the *Italia* whose bridge had been damaged by a German bomb on 9 September 1943.

DOCUMENT No. III

The Royal Italian Air Force

1. WHAT IT HAS DONE

AFTER the events immediately succeeding the publication of the armistice, the Air Force consisted of:

> 115 fighters.
> 90 bombers and transport planes.
> 50 seaplanes.
> 50 planes of various types.
> ——
> 305

The ground organization was still efficient in the Puglie and in Sardinia; in the other provinces it was practically non-existent. The greater part of the indispensable industrial plants for the construction and maintenance of the planes were in central and northern Italy under the control of the Germans.

In spite of its meagre resources the Italian Air Force between

8 September 1943 and 15 April 1944, carried out the following
duties:

Hours of flight	12,500
Number of sorties	9,444
Bombs dropped	40,000
Rounds fired	100,000
Supplies dropped	150,000 kg.
Sea rescues and wounded transported .	119
Mails and *matériel* carried . . .	900,000 kg.
Miles flown	350,000

In the course of these duties under the strict control and
limitations of all kinds imposed by the Allied Control Commission, the Italian Air Force carried out the following operations:

1. Bombing raids, cannon and machine-gun attacks, and
   reconnaissance flights in the Balkan peninsula (eastern
   zone). In Montenegro more than 100 military vehicles
   were destroyed.
2. Anti-submarine patrols and searches for wrecks in the
   Ionian Sea and the Adriatic.
3. Transport of men and supplies to the Italian troops and
   the Partisans fighting in Montenegro, and the maintenance of regular communications between the Italian
   mainland, the Islands, and North Africa.

In these operations the losses in personnel between 8 September 1943 and 15 April 1944 were 80 killed, 46 missing.

The work of the Italian Air Force was warmly praised by
Air Vice-Marshal Foster, Head of the Air Sub-commission of
the Allied Control Commission, in a message on his departure
from Italy in March of this year. *The Times* of 25 April 1944
published an article describing the achievements of the Italian
Air Force in the face of all difficulties. Mr. Churchill in his
speech in the House of Commons on 24 May 1944 said: 'The
loyal Italian Air Force has also fought so well that I am making
special efforts to supply them with improved aircraft of British
manufacture.'

It should be emphasized that in all these activities nothing but Italian *matériel* was used.

2. WHAT IT MIGHT HAVE DONE

The activities of the Italian Air Force have been limited by the Allied air authorities, and strictly controlled by the Allied Control Commission, which laid down that the Italian Air Force should only operate in the Balkan zone. All plans had first to be submitted to the Head of the Air Sub-commission of the Allied Control Commission, so that instead of being merely controlled, the Italian Air Force came under the direct orders of the Allied Control Commission. The Italian High Command and the Air Command were deprived of all freedom of action. In addition, the Allied Control Commission prohibited the use of Italian bombers on offensive operations, and also for many months prohibited the use of wireless communications between airfields, and even between airfields and aeroplanes in the air.

The planes used were of an obsolete type, and owing to the lack of repairs and spare parts their efficiency left much to be desired. After 8 September 1943, owing to the lack of industrial plants in southern Italy and the failure of the Allies to provide any *matériel*, the planes were kept fit for service only by a patient and ingenious use of existing *matériel* and by the recovery of spare parts from old machines in Sicily, Sardinia, and North Africa.

The Italian Air Force had a large number of pilots and mechanics of great professional ability who could have been employed, and who could have serviced Allied planes and equipment. The Italian personnel available at the time (pilots, technical officers, mechanics, and ground crews) could have provided crews for 1,100 aircraft (60 per cent. fighters, 30 per cent. bombers, 10 per cent. seaplanes). If the 500 pilots then prisoners of war in Allied hands had been released, personnel would have been available for another 500, making a total of 1,500 aeroplanes.

DOCUMENT No. IV

The Government and the Patriots

IT has been pointed out that the whole of the Italian people were opposed to the war, and that they never made any secret of their feelings. The coldness with which the Germans were treated concealed a hatred which found no public expression. The German troops in Italy behaved extremely well; they had very little to do with the people, and gave no trouble.

The first sign that the atmosphere had changed was given by the troops who poured into the country after 25 July; they were insolent and contemptuous, though they still behaved correctly, but after 8 September they behaved as if they were in a conquered country, an attitude which was one of the causes of the resistance movement. This developed in many different ways until the groups were organized, and could co-ordinate their activities with the operations of the Allies.

The first information received by the Government described the movement as being very widespread. There followed news of a reduction in its numbers, this was due partly to the relative tranquillity which reigned after the first few days in the area controlled by the Nazis and the Fascists, and partly owing to disappointment over the slowness of the Allied advance. The defections which occurred meant the disappearance of many undesirable elements, whose presence had made the work of organization extremely dangerous.

The Government immediately recognized the potential value of the movement and the importance of not allowing the different groups to collapse for lack of support, and for lack of leadership to co-ordinate their efforts. First of all it was essential to establish contacts between the various organizations which had taken the field, between them and our own High Command, and between them and the Allies. This task was entrusted to missions composed almost entirely of men from the armed forces; they reached the occupied territory in many ways; slipping through the enemy lines. being landed by surface ships and submarines on the Adriatic and Tyrrhenian coasts, and being dropped from aeroplanes.

From October 1943 to May 1944 twenty-six missions were sent to occupied territory, of which twenty-two were provided with wireless sets, and four were to carry out special acts of sabotage. The wireless liaison missions sent and received 1,232 messages during that period, making it possible to keep in touch with fifty-four more or less organized groups. It was also possible to obtain accurate information about the enemy, and to ascertain the most pressing needs of the Patriots. In order to send supplies it was first of all necessary to arrange for areas in every region where they could be dropped or landed. By the end of May these 'reception camps' as they were called, numbered 129.

In January the first deliveries took place. Usually a single plane dropped a ton and a half in special containers. There were Sten guns, *matériel* needed for sabotage and for incendiary purposes, hand grenades, provisions, clothes, medicines, and comforts. In May 99 flights were made and 174 tons were dropped. During April the first machine-guns were dropped.

᠁᠁   ᠁᠁   ᠁᠁

The Patriots responded enthusiastically to the efforts that the Government made on their behalf. Although the winter was chiefly a period of recruitment and organization, the Patriots carried out many acts of sabotage. This was essentially the work of individuals, who showed such determination that they created a permanent state of alarm. During March and April the German High Command organized throughout the occupied territory large-scale operations with considerable forces, which had to be withdrawn from the front line.

From documents in the possession of the Italian High Command it is possible to give the following accurate, but incomplete, account of the activities of the Patriots:

101 attacks on Germans and Fascists, or on industrial establishments which they had occupied, actions which led to armed encounters;

o

75 attacks by the enemy on the Patriots in the course of mopping-up operations;

142 attacks on individual Nazis and Fascists, which caused the elimination of elements opposed to the national cause;

155 acts of sabotage against railways, roads, telegraph lines, industrial establishments, dumps, and supply columns.

When the spring offensive opened the Allied forces found bands of Patriots in existence everywhere, or in the course of being formed. It was thus possible to use these groups in central Italy and to co-ordinate their activities with the operations of the British and American troops.

⟶   ⟶   ⟶

This is only a summary of what has been done by the Patriots. The true story can only be written when the reports of each organization have been examined and checked. They will demonstrate the love of the Italians for their country and their determination to cleanse it from the Nazi-Fascist stain.

DOCUMENT No. V

The Prisoners of War

I IMMEDIATELY felt that the question of the prisoners of war was of the very greatest importance owing to their immense numbers, their dispersal in so many parts of the world, and the effects of the prolonged confinement which caused great anxiety to their families and had such an enervating effect on the prisoners themselves.

In the beginning I tried to handle this difficult matter myself, but I soon found that it was too complicated, that it needed too much study; I was busy from morning to night with the varied and always pressing tasks of the Head of the Government, and I could not give it the attention it needed. I therefore decided to ask General Mason-MacFarlane to obtain the repatriation of General Gazzera, who was a prisoner

in the United States. I have always had the greatest admira-
tion for this officer, who combines great intelligence with the
highest sense of duty, and an extraordinary capacity for work.
With the consent of the Council of Ministers, I appointed him
High Commissioner for Prisoners, setting out his duties in an
Order in Council. The best way of explaining what has been
done for our prisoners is to print the summary which General
Gazzera prepared for my successor, Signor Bonomi.

There is an extremely large number of Italian prisoners, and
the relevant data which were gradually compiled in Rome is
not in our possession. At the moment we have only the following figures, which have been collected with great difficulty and
are only approximate:

Great Britain: 360,000 prisoners, divided as follows: England
and Scotland, 75,000; India and Ceylon, 60,000; Near
East, 60,000; East Africa, 60,000; North Africa, 45,000;
South Africa, 45,000; Australia, 10,000; West Africa,
5,000.

United States: 90,000 prisoners, divided as follows: America,
50,000; North Africa, 40,000.

Russia: 70,000 prisoners.

France: 40,000 prisoners in North Africa.

Germany: 450,000 prisoners.

As regards the length of imprisonment, the figures can
approximately be divided as follows:

More than three years . . .	80,000
From two to three years . .	140,000
About two years	110,000
About one year	230,000
About nine months . . .	450,000
	1,010,000

To this number must be added about 20,000 interned in
Switzerland, and some hundreds in Hungary, Roumania, and
Turkey.

With regard to the prisoners captured before the armistice, the large number may perhaps be explained by the nature of this war, in which armoured formations and air forces are able to isolate great masses; in our case this was rendered easier by our great inferiority in weapons and services. This was especially and tragically evident in Ethiopia, where all the men, whether called up for service or not, who were not killed, were captured and treated as prisoners of war.

Except for a few individual cases of cowardice, which must be dealt with eventually for the honour of Italy, the mass of the prisoners did their duty to the limits of human endurance. The Italian soldier fought uncomplainingly despite the lack of weapons, equipment, and rations. Perhaps few other soldiers would have fought under such deplorable conditions. The officers tried by every means in their power, and above all by their own example, to make good the deficiencies in equipment.

With regard to the conditions in the camps, it may be stated that the treatment of prisoners in the hands of the British (except for certain differences in different regions) is good on the whole, conforming to the conditions laid down in the Geneva Convention.

The treatment of those in American hands also conforms to the Convention and may be described as good, or very good, except in the matter of pay and allowances.

Nothing positive is known of the number and the treatment of the mass of the prisoners in Russian hands; in February urgent representations were made to M. Vishinsky to obtain information about the number, names, and condition of the Italian prisoners; the same request was made on 16 May. Up to the present no reply has been received. Signor Togliatti reports that the officers and men were well treated in the camp which he visited; he also says that three Italian generals had been captured, and that there had been a large number of deaths from illness among the prisoners.

Until a short time ago the prisoners in French hands in

North Africa have been treated extremely badly; they suffered from hunger, lack of clothing, and even from actual cruelty. Repeated protests in Algiers and here have, it seems, recently[1] obtained some improvement in conditions. It should be noted that the Allied High Command, whose troops captured these prisoners, is responsible for these grave violations of human rights. Our Government has taken steps to try to arrange that all prisoners of war in North Africa should be in British or American hands, and it appears that almost 2,000 men have been transferred. The Government is doing all that it can to send food and clothing from America to these unfortunate men. (The Allied Control Commission has prevented the sending of such supplies from Italy owing to the scarcity of these commodities; it has only allowed the dispatch of books and small objects for personal use.)

Our prisoners in Germany have suffered and are suffering from hunger and cold; the officers are in a worse plight than the other ranks, who are working for firms or private individuals. The greatest pressure is put on all prisoners to make them submit to the so-called Fascist Republic. It appears that Germany only recognizes as 'prisoners of war' (and therefore protected by the Geneva Convention), those who were captured when fighting with the Allies; it regards as 'military internees' (and therefore not protected by the Convention) those who were arrested at the time of the armistice. The Government has recently asked for assistance from the Vatican and the International Red Cross in arranging for food and clothing to be sent from America to our prisoners of war in Germany.

From the point of view of morale, imprisonment has a very debilitating effect on men if they are not naturally energetic; most of them, unhappy at having been captured, become irritable and suspicious; the lack, the irregularity, and the scarcity of news from their homes and from Italy, render them pessimistic and depressed; the weaker characters are easily influenced by propaganda and the wildest rumours. In addi-

[1] The spring of 1944. (*Translator.*)

tion, as the Geneva Convention of 27 July 1929 (the 'charter' which governs the lives of prisoners) has implicitly allowed the separation of officers and other ranks, the bonds of discipline are weakened, making internal and external propaganda more effective. But their fundamental good sense has shown itself in the characteristic qualities of the Italian soldier—discipline and resourcefulness.

It is, however, true that the armistice caused many disturbances in camps where there were no leaders ready to explain the situation; it is also true that the inopportune and inadequate work of the Allied authorities in trying to track down 'Fascists', has accentuated, if it has not introduced, political distinctions into the camps. In every military organism politics invariably endanger discipline and cause disputes and quarrels. However, the great majority of the prisoners in British and American hands are ready, as always, to obey the legitimate Italian Government. Spontaneous expressions of loyalty reach this country from our troops in different prison camps.

  ∿   ∿   ∿

The Geneva Convention lays down (Article 2) that prisoners of war are to be treated with respect; (Article 31) that they are not to undertake any work directly connected with the conduct of the war, particularly in the manufacture and transport of arms or munitions of any kind, or in the transport of supplies for the combatant units.

After the armistice the Allies decided that our men were to remain prisoners. But under co-belligerency the Allies asked if the prisoners could be employed in the rear areas, to which the Head of the Government necessarily agreed in principle, while waiting for detailed agreements between the Allied and the Italian High Commands, as Italy has always desired to give the greatest possible support to the armed forces of the co-belligerents. On the basis of this general agreement, the British military authorities, declaring that they were working in full agreement with the Italian Government, tried to induce the prisoners in many camps to state in writing that they were

willing to undertake any work, even if it were forbidden by
the Geneva Convention, while still remaining prisoners, though
under improved conditions. In this way the Allies formed a
certain number of units with Italian officers and non-com-
missioned officers, but commanded and administered by British
officers, thus violating the Geneva Convention and infringing
the Italian military code.

The American military authorities, while behaving in the
same way in Morocco and Algiers, were prevented from doing
so in America, because the senior general in their hands
pointed out the irregularity of the action they were about to
take. As a result of his representations, they discussed with
him the formation of purely Italian units, which would have
been consonant with our dignity as Italians and soldiers. These
units would have served as pioneer troops with the American
forces, or been trained and armed as combatants. This plan
was embodied in an agreement to be submitted for approval
by the British and Italian Governments.

Instead of this, a proposal was presented in January 1944
to the Italian Government, which, had it been accepted, would
have transformed our prisoners into labourers under the command of the United Nations in any part of the world, to be
employed on work considered useful in the common interest.
The proposal was naturally rejected with indignation by the
Head of the Government, who suggested instead that the
question should be considered by an Anglo-American-Italian
Commission. With this in mind a High Commissioner for
Prisoners was appointed at the beginning of March and his
duties were laid down in the *R.D.L.* of 6 April 1944, no. 107.

In the second half of March the Allied Control Commission
issued a new decree, declaring that the details, but not the
substance, were open to discussion. Reserving our right to
be treated on a basis of equality, there were some meetings
between the High Commissioner and General Mason-Mac-
Farlane and then with the Head of the Government. We
presented a counter-proposal with the object of making use
of our prisoners in the armed forces against the common

enemy, but safeguarding at least a minimum of Italian military organization and our national dignity. As no agreement was reached the negotiations were suspended, and General Mason-MacFarlane submitted the question to the British and American Governments. The proposal and the counter-proposal may be summarized as follows:

A. The American and British Governments demanded that Italian soldiers, although they were co-belligerents and although they were obliged to renounce their rights under the Geneva Convention, were to remain prisoners of war. The Italian Government demanded that all Italian soldiers should cease to be regarded as prisoners of war.

B. The American and British Governments demanded that units should be commanded by American and British officers. The Italian Government was naturally determined that in theory and in practice the units should be commanded by Italian officers, even if the units were working with the Allied forces.

In addition, the Italian Government was determined that all the prisoners were to be organized in formations not smaller than a battalion; the two Allied Governments by use of an ambiguous phrase wished to reserve their liberty of action, which would have allowed differences in the treatment of our prisoners and the breaking up of our formations with damage to their morale and discipline.

C. The Allied Control Commission asked that a similar agreement should be reached separately with the French Committee of Liberation. The Italian Government agreed in order to obviate certain difficulties.

D. The Allied Control Commission made no reference to our prisoners of war in Russia, and the Government reserved its right to treat this question separately with a Russian representative; up to the present this has not been done.

The negotiations had reached this point when the Italian Government learned with great surprise from a communication in *Stars and Stripes* and through an announcement by the B.B.C. on the same day, that Italian troops were being organized in special pioneer units under the command of Allied officers, while still remaining prisoners of war.

A very strong letter of remonstrance from the President of the Council, dated 10 May, immediately asked for official information, recapitulating the course of the negotiations, giving a list of the violations of the Geneva Convention in this statement, and insisting on the duty of the Italian Government 'to protect its nationals, their status as prisoners and, even more, their honour as soldiers'.

General Mason-MacFarlane stated on 18 May that he had forwarded this letter to the Allied High Command at Algiers asking for an immediate answer. Up to the present no reply has been received.

Meanwhile the following facts have emerged:

In Sicily there are two prisoner of war camps with about 9,000 prisoners; other officers and men are at liberty on parole, which formula came to our knowledge on the 12th of this month.[1] This is inadmissible for it obliges our men to fail in their duty and to commit crimes as defined in Articles 217 and 218 of the military penal code. The following units or individuals have been transferred from North Africa to Italy, but, however, remain prisoners of war with the others:

One company of workers to Bari (637th Italian Pioneer Company) who are employed in various ways in support of combatant troops.

In December 150 officers were sent to Sicily to organize pioneer companies.

At the beginning of May 170 officers were landed at Naples, were sent for some days to a prisoners' camp at Aversa and then sent to form other pioneer companies in Sicily.

[1] June 1944. (*Translator.*)

Veterinary officers were attached to Allied military units, while remaining prisoners.

In Sicily American police units, pioneer, transport, and other service units were formed of prisoners, who retained that status.

Italian prisoners of war of unknown origin, rank, and branch of the services, are employed here and there on the mainland in different Allied commands as waiters, cooks, &c. for nationals of other countries, while remaining prisoners of war.

Protests have already been made to the Allied Control Commission against some of these actions which are legally and morally indefensible. Up to the present the following results have been obtained:

Prisoners in Sicily have gradually been released by the Allied military authorities and by the High Commissioner for urgent reasons of health or on compassionate grounds.

Prisoners on the mainland have been released for urgent reasons of health or on compassionate grounds.

But in my opinion it is necessary and urgent to take the most energetic steps to obtain the release of all Italian prisoners, immorally and illegally still retained by the Allies on national territory, despite co-belligerency. I am repeating in writing my verbal request to the Allied Control Commission that this should be done.

The wounded, the seriously ill and disabled prisoners are being sent back, a few at a time, on the recommendation of the International Medical Commissions. A few, a very few, able-bodied prisoners asked for by name by the Government for urgent military reasons are being released. A certain number of officers and other ranks were repatriated in this way; then the Allied Control Commission announced that the Allies would only release another 150 men on these grounds, on the basis of successive batches of 25, the next 25 only being released when the 25 on the preceding list had arrived; three lists have been sent but only 5 prisoners have been released.

We have recently forwarded a memorandum asking that the oldest prisoners and those who have been longest in Allied hands should be sent home; so far we have only obtained a promise of the release of prisoners for urgent family reasons.

I now propose to ask for the release of prisoners who are indispensable for the work of the civil administration; I am approaching the President of the Council with a view to the drawing up of a memorandum for future action.

Those prisoners who have been repatriated have raised many complicated legal and financial questions between the Italian Government and the Allied Powers. The Geneva Convention lays down (Article 24) that before a prisoner is sent home he must receive any pay due to him from the detaining Power. Up to the present the Allies have sent these men back with a credit note, telling them that they would receive the sum due to them from the Italian Government. This is an obvious and grave violation of the Convention; it imposes a serious strain on Italian finances and great hardship on the prisoners.

I am taking steps to obtain a satisfactory settlement in this matter.

DOCUMENT No. VI

Internal Reconstruction

AFTER 10 September the King, the Head of the Government, the Ministers of Marine, Air, and subsequently the Minister of Industry, Commerce, and Labour were all on liberated territory, thus providing a *de jure* and *de facto* Government, sufficient in numbers to prove the continued existence of the Italian State, beyond the grasp of the German octopus. But this Government had to face on the one hand the Allies, who were naturally suspicious, and on the other a population which was demoralized and embittered. A mere declaration of survival was not enough to inspire confidence, it had to be accompanied by measures which would show that the handful of ministers was able and determined to carry out the tasks which lay in front of them. Vigorous action was necessary not only in the interests of the country, but also to escape from the degrading role of a 'puppet Government'.

'Action' was the 'Order of the Day' among the leaders in that remote corner of Italy, which was all that remained of the national territory. Sustained by little more than an undying faith in the future of their country, they began the work of reconstruction, which perhaps will take a generation to complete.

But the will of the State is created and expresses itself through many complex organisms, which the 'Men of Brindisi' did not possess, even in embryo. Here, therefore, was the first objective—to organize a government, with hardly any trained personnel and amid almost insurmountable difficulties. It was both a baffling problem and an inescapable necessity. The few civil servants available were forced to limit their work to the most urgent tasks, while they were without guidance and control owing to the lack of a central organ of government. Even before the war the local financial and business firms had been reduced almost to bankruptcy by the former régime, and could not meet the demands on their resources caused by the state of emergency. Only forty-five days after the collapse of Fascism most of them were in danger of being forced into liquidation. Many of the banks, the semi-state organizations, and the great industrial undertakings, had their head offices and boards of directors in occupied territory; deprived of their chairmen they were legally unable to take any action. The railways, even where they had not been destroyed by the Germans, were paralysed, the other means of communication were interrupted, public officials had disappeared, private enterprise was reduced to providing for the most elementary needs of the population. Such were the almost insoluble difficulties which confronted the Government.

⚬   ⚬   ⚬

Collecting the few experienced civil servants who were available, I set up an 'Office of Civil Affairs', which, under the dynamic and able administration of Signor Innocenti, began its work on 14 September. It dealt with all questions within the competence of the Government, except the armed forces. Only the self-sacrifice and devotion of its staff enabled this office to carry out its varied and complicated duties. Thanks largely to the ability of Signor Spinelli, the President of the Brindisi Law Courts, the work was so well organized that it was possible to sub-divide it between the different departments as these were set up; the first as I have already explained, being Foreign Affairs and Finance.

The optimism which prevailed in Allied circles was shared by most Italians; it encouraged them not only to put up with every discomfort, but also gave a purely temporary character to this microcosm of government and limited its activities to the necessities of the moment. However, as Italians gradually learned that the optimism about the rapid liberation of Italy was exaggerated, the Office of Civil Affairs realized that it must take a more long-term view of its duties and began a proper reorganization of the administration and finances of the liberated territory. It had to deal with reconstruction on a national basis, while continuing to face and solve local problems relating to the small extent of territory which was under its control—that is to say the provinces of Bari, Brindisi, Lecce, Taranto, Cagliari, Nuoro, and Sassari.

While getting into touch with the authorities in those zones and awaiting the indispensable work of readjustment, I considered it desirable to confer the widest powers allowed by law on the Prefects, to ensure that there were no obstacles in the way of maintaining order, and to inspire confidence through the normal working of the public services. With this object in view the prefects were allowed to order all civil servants who were absent from their usual offices to present themselves for employment. The prefects were given powers to order the resumption of payments by certain banks, which had blocked all accounts; payments were also authorized in necessitous cases, such as those to the families of civil servants who were in occupied territory, or who had been removed to Germany, and to war orphans. Arrangements were made for refugees who were arriving in increasing numbers from the zone of operations, and steps were taken to reopen the schools.

In order to reassure the Allies on the good faith of the Government, I gave orders that public order must be maintained in the rear areas, and that dangerous Fascists were to be arrested. I forbade the formation of irresponsible bands of volunteers, more especially as those who really wished to fight could join the regular army. The democratic character of the Government was emphasized in every possible way, among others by the announcement of its intention to abrogate the so-called 'racial legislation' and to restore all their rights as citizens to the Jews, and by the removal of Fascists from public offices and the beginning of the 'purge'.

But the circular letters through which I communicated these plans, if they provided a rapid means of getting into touch with the local authorities, were insufficient to give the country that legal framework which every day became more urgently needed. The defective working of the Government prevented the issue of the usual *Decreti-leggi*, so that the only practical method was to avail myself of the power to issue Orders (*Bandi*), conferred on the Supreme Commander of the Armed Forces by the Laws of War.[1]

This power was at first exercised directly by the King as the Supreme Commander; but later it was delegated to the Chief of the General Staff,[2] so that such legislative activity should not create suspicions of absolutism, and the Crown would be absolved from all responsibility, in accordance with the principles of the Constitution.

The circulation of money was regulated by an Order[3] so as to meet the temporary lack of currency after the run on the banks. As the result of a conference of the Directors of the

[1] Articles 16 and 17 of the annex to *R.D.*, 8 July 1938, no. 1415, which refers to the laws of war and neutrality.

[2] *Bando del Re*, no. 187—A.C. 30 September 1943.

[3] *Bando del Re*, no. 38—A.C. 21 September 1943.

Bank of Italy in Puglia it happened that after 13 September 162 millions of lire had arrived in Bari for exceptional expenses; they had, fortunately, been sent from Rome a week before the armistice. The currency at the branches of the Bank of Issue in the Puglie amounted to about half a milliard, which was hardly sufficient to meet the ordinary withdrawals and the needs of the Treasury up to the end of November. The experts, having suggested some expedients, did not conceal their anxiety about the situation, and it was therefore necessary to give provisional instructions that drafts issued by the Bank of Italy and other banks covered by their capital resources, and officially stamped, should be accepted as legal currency.

The knowledge that the banks were solvent and that all future demands would be met, increased the confidence of the Allies, and prevented hoarding of currency. These exceptional regulations were only in force for a short time owing to the reappearance of the ordinary currency and to the circulation of the Allied occupation issue. The use of stamped drafts was soon abandoned, while those already in circulation were withdrawn.

The danger of a crisis from the lack of money in circulation had hardly passed when, with the dizzy increase in prices, the opposite phenomenon made its appearance. This was due to the amount of money spent by the troops and the Allied Commands and the deplorable course of the exchange. The Government was unable to control this excess of money in circulation—and who knows for how long, and in what quantities, it will continue to undermine the impoverished economy of our country? All that the Government could do was to try to direct the flow of this superabundant money to the Bank of Issue through the banks, and with that object to encourage the establishment of subsidiary savings banks offering particularly advantageous terms to depositors. Inflation was therefore kept within bounds, at the same time providing the State with more reliable resources than those which would have been obtained from the problematical issue of loans.

Directly connected with monetary problems which for obvious reasons led to the 'black market', there were the problems of food. Owing to the scarcity of food and the paralysis of communications, there were innumerable buying organizations, each acting independently; the Army, the Navy, and the Air Force were competing against each other, while the prefects—who were faced with the greatest difficulties—struggled to deal with the situation through the Provincial Food Offices. I daily received the most pessimistic reports and desperate appeals for help.

An equal distribution of available supplies could only be assured by the setting up of a single organization provided with the necessary funds so as to be able to act quickly, so a Commissioner-General for Food was appointed[1] and attached to the Department of the Quartermaster-General. His duty was to provide for the needs of the civilian population as well as the armed forces, making use of military lorries which were placed at his disposal. To supplement the other inadequate means of transport a series of regulations were issued for the utilization of merchant shipping: all ships over 300 tons were commandeered;[2] the harbour masters were authorized to make loans to captains of merchant ships;[3] insurance was undertaken by the Government for war risks for sailing-ships with auxiliary motors, and for their cargoes;[4] the rate of pay for the crews of requisitioned ships, not on the register of the auxiliary navy, was laid down;[5] indemnities for war risks were increased by 250 per cent.[6]

Orders were issued which dealt with the most urgent and varied matters—some economic, such as the stamping of bank drafts and the money orders needed by public departments; some legal, such as the moratorium on private and public

[1] *Bando del Capo di Stato Maggiore Generale*, no. 284, 1 October 1943.
[2] Ibid., no. 2, 7 October 1943.
[3] Ibid., no. 3, 8 October 1943.
[4] Ibid., no. 10, 4 November 1943.
[5] Ibid., no. 11, 4 November 1943.
[6] Ibid., no. 12, 6 November 1943.

debts, for the suspension of the Statute of Limitations, for the postponement of trials, &c.

All this work was carried on in conjunction with the Allied authorities with whom the Office of Civil Affairs maintained cordial relations.

      ·◇·   ·◇·   ·◇·

The hope of the early liberation of Rome faded with the passing of time, while the extent of the territory under the control of the Government increased. More machinery had to be set up to administer the provinces efficiently and so increase the prestige of the Cabinet. To govern without the appropriate legislation became impossible, especially in regard to the budget, and there were in addition urgent matters such as appointments, promotions, &c.

In these circumstances it was decided to issue an Order conferring on the Cabinet the power to make laws, such legislation to be strictly limited in scope because it would not be in accordance with the principles of the Constitution. The transference of the functions of the central government to regional bodies during a state of war was open to a similar objection; it would have been inopportune not only because of the difficulties of decentralization, but also because of the impossibility of dealing with the problem as a whole.

In fact, in view of the gradual restoration of normal conditions in the territory administered by the Italian Government, the legality of government by decree (which had been necessary during a state of emergency) became more and more doubtful, and proved the need to create a Cabinet with powers to carry out its proper functions. Having failed in my efforts to induce the representatives of the different political parties to assume the responsibilities of government, nothing remained but to appoint experts, as I have already explained. To maintain the 'apostolic succession' I proposed that the new members of the Government should be appointed as under-secretaries so that the ministers, who had remained in Rome, should still be regarded as holding office.

P

It was, however, necessary to remove all the other obstacles in substance and in form, which still obstructed the work of the Government. I therefore issued a series of laws in order to confer on the under-secretaries the right to sit in the Council of Ministers;[1] to confer on the Head of the Government the functions of the Lord Privy Seal, to affix the Seal to laws and decrees during the absence of the Minister;[2] to suspend temporarily the law making it obligatory to ask the approval of the Council of State and other consultative bodies before affixing the Seal, and the registration with the *Corte dei Conti*[3] of the adaptation of the formula for the laws now issued; the publication of a special series of the Official Gazette of the Realm.[4] As I wished to obviate any doubts in the minds of the Allies as to the loyalty of the Italian Government, I removed from the signature of acts signed in the name of the King, the reference to the sovereignty of Albania and Ethiopia.

The form chosen for this legislation and for what followed was that of *decreti-leggi* in conformity with that adopted in Rome from 25 July to 8 September 1943. Before the under-secretaries assumed office certain urgent laws had to be issued: to deal with the crisis of the lack of accommodation caused by the destruction of houses in the fighting and increased by requisitioning, and to give protection to lodgers threatened with eviction;[5] to protect the interests of those who in person or juridically were resident in territory occupied by the enemy, making it possible to nominate special custodians or commissioners for the sub-offices, branches, or agencies of firms and enterprises whose headquarters were in occupied territory.[6]

With the active participation of the under-secretaries the government departments began to work more efficiently and it was possible to organize more collaboration with the Allies

---

[1] *R.D.L.*, 10 November 1943, no. 5B.
[2] *R.D.L.*, 30 October 1943, no. 1B.
[3] *R.D.L.*, 30 October 1943, no. 2B.
[4] *R.D.L.*, 30 October 1943, no. 3B.
[5] *R.D.L.*, 11 November 1943, no. 6B.
[6] *R.D.L.*, 15 November 1943, no. 8B.

through the Allied Control Commission which was set up on
10 November 1943 by the Allied Commander-in-Chief in the
Mediterranean.

◇   ◇   ◇

When the new members of the Government took office they
were able to establish their own departments. The secretariat
of the Cabinet was separated from the Office of Civil Affairs,
which in the meantime had enjoyed the assistance of an able
official, Signor Bilancia, who after many adventures had managed to slip through the enemy's lines. Signor Innocenti, with
his inexhaustible energy, became director of the secretariat.
This office, after awaiting the provisional organization of the
various departments, supervised their work; it was strength-
ened by the arrival from Naples of Signor Medugno, a distinguished constitutional lawyer. It studied and drafted the
necessary legislation, exercised the control normally exercised
by the Office of the Lord Privy Seal, acted on behalf of other
departments in the drafting of laws which needed particular
legal and administrative experience, collaborating with the
offices of other ministers to fill the gap left by the absence of
the Council of State and other consultative bodies.

In accordance with the line of policy discussed by the Council
of Ministers in its first plenary session,[1] the Cabinet, while

---

[1] At the meeting on 24 November 1943 the Council of Ministers approved and published the following statement:

'The Council of Ministers, in response to the popular demand for a
return to the glorious liberal traditions of the *Risorgimento* and to constitutional practice, and to the demand for sanctions, legal, political, administrative and moral against those responsible for the subversion of the State, for
the present military and political situation brought about against the feelings,
the wishes and the interests of the nation, and for the twenty years of an
illegal dictatorship, will take the necessary steps to implement this declaration of policy:

'1. The Council of Ministers declares that the Fascists responsible for
the suppression of public and individual liberty, are unworthy to exercise
political rights.

'2. The Council of Ministers suspends from to-day until three months

recognizing that it consisted of experts, did not hesitate to undertake the task of democratizing and purging the government departments in accordance with the popular demand. As the carrying out of the published programme was in part the work of the succeeding Cabinet (which with a different label was almost the same in compostion) I shall, in order to save space, give an account of the activities of the Ministry which took office on 11 February 1944.

In a short space of time the following laws were drafted and approved:

Disbanding of the Fascist Militia for reasons of national security.[1]

after the declaration of peace, the Statute of Limitations for crimes not of a political nature.

'3. The Council of Ministers will review all the contracts or concessions harmful to the rights or interests of the State, of public and semi-state bodies, granted by political pressure.

'4. The Council of Ministers will review all the legislation of the last twenty years to bring it into line with the principles of the Italian tradition of justice, a revision already begun with the abolition of the death sentence, the racial laws and the laws which limit family rights.

'5. The Council of Ministers declares that all who show cowardice in the face of the enemy, Fascists who have engaged in fratricidal strife, committed attacks on persons, or in any way collaborated with the German troops or authorities after the declaration of the armistice, will be tried by military courts.

'6. The Council of Ministers will abolish the Fascist Militia.

'7. The Council of Ministers annuls appointments and promotions made for political reasons, and will remove from the Government service all members of the Fascist Fighting Squads, participants of the March on Rome, wearers of the "Lictor's Scarf" and Fascist officials known to be guilty of attacks on individual liberty.

'8. The Council of Ministers will reinstate in the government service those who have been dismissed for political reasons, and will examine all cases where promotion was refused for political reasons.

'9. The Council of Ministers will remove from the public service all Fascists whose proved political antecedents unfit them for service in the present situation and a state of war. None of these sanctions will be applied to those who have redeemed their past in the struggle against the common enemy.'

[1] *R.D.L.*, 6 December 1943, no. 16B.

Elimination from the public administration of those connected with the former régime.[1]

Removal of inequalities between citizens created by the
Fascists by the readmission to the public services of those
dismissed for political reasons,[2] and by the abrogation of
all racial legislation with the consequent granting to the
Jews of all civil, political, and family rights.[3]

At the same time a detailed study was made for the revision
of all laws affecting the status of civil servants who had been
promoted or degraded through political influence, and for the
revision of all concessions and contracts harmful to the public
service obtained by political influence.

In the meantime, as I have said, the punishment of those
responsible for the Fascist tyranny and for the national catastrophe, and the confiscation for the benefit of the State of the
illegal profits acquired under the Fascist régime were being
dealt with by the necessary legislation. But the proceedings
gave rise to difficult administrative and legal problems and
aroused the most burning public interest, kept alive by a
frenzied press campaign, until the appointment of a High
Commissioner for the Purge[4] created the necessary machinery,
and improved the morale of the country.

჻   ჻   ჻

The Allies who during this period had received proof of
the loyal co-operation of the Italian Government, and had had
an opportunity to appreciate the value of its contribution, were
willing to hand over the southern provinces and the Islands
to Italian administration. At the same time the decision to
transfer the Government to Salerno was agreed to by the Allied
Control Commission, who accepted my condition that the

[1] *R.D.L.*, 28 December 1943, no. 29B, incorporated in *R.D.L.*, 12 April
1943, no. 101.

[2] *R.D.L.*, 6 January, 1943, no. 9, incorporated in *R.D.L.*, 12 April 1943,
no. 101.

[3] *R.D.L.*, 20 January 1943, nos. 25 and 26.

[4] *R.D.L.*, 13 April 1944, no. 110.

province of Salerno should also be handed over. It would have meant a great loss of prestige if the seat of the Government had not been under Italian administration.

Notwithstanding the lack of means at our disposal, the transfer was carried out in an orderly manner and without any interruption in the work of the Government. It brought many advantages such as a better centre in regard to the territory to be administered and the better organization of the central administration. During the preceding period it had been impossible to concentrate all the departments at Brindisi;[1] even still, some of them could not find accommodation at Salerno, which had been largely destroyed, while many of the remaining buildings had been requisitioned by the Allies.[2]

At Brindisi, as at Salerno and in other cities where the government departments were established, the local authorities and the residents were most friendly and hospitable, smoothing out small but annoying difficulties, and maintaining public order so as not to add to the arduous work of the Government.

The immediate object of the reconstituted Government was the carrying out of the agreements for the taking over of the restored provinces, agreements which were embodied in laws. The first of these[3] laid down that the exercise of all the powers of the State was resumed by the Italian Government from zero hour on 11 February 1944 in the territory lying south of the northern limits of the provinces of Salerno, Potenza, and Bari, in Sicily and the adjacent islands, except Pantelleria, Lampedusa, and Linosa. The second[4] regulated the legal system in those territories, laying down that from the same date, the

[1] The Ministry of War and a large part of the Ministry of Internal Affairs were at Lecce; the Ministry of Marine was at Taranto, while the Ministries of Justice, Agriculture, Public Works, Air, and the Under-Secretary for Railways were at Bari.

[2] The Ministries of War, Marine, Air, Industry, as well as the Under-Secretaries of the Mercantile Marine and of the Railways were unable to find accommodation at Salerno and were respectively at Lecce, Taranto, Bari, Vietri sul Mare, and Naples.

[3] *R.D.L.*, 11 February 1944, no. 30.

[4] *R.D.L.*, 11 February 1944, no. 31.

ordinances of the Allied Military Administration ceased to be valid, while legalizing all action previously taken. The third[1] stabilized the wages paid to workers, fixed the maximum prices for all kinds of property and services, and authorized the Head of the Government to issue regulations with regard to production, and the Minister of Finance to sequestrate and administer properties and firms which were controlled directly or indirectly by Fascist interests or by persons who were in prison or legally of enemy nationality.

Subsequently, as the result of laborious negotiations, it was possible to improve many of the agreements, notably the one which dealt with the competence of the Allied military authorities to try according to Italian law persons accused of hostile acts or crimes committed in liberated territory against the Allied forces, or officials or representatives of the United Nations. Shortly afterwards we succeeded in restoring to the Italian courts the right to try such cases, the Allied courts reserving their right, however, to try the cases if they so determined.[2]

All efforts to obtain a revision of the rates of wages to be paid to workers and employees were in vain. The Government fully realized the disastrous consequences, but were unable to give any practical sign of their sympathy.

One step towards the return to democratic institutions was the re-establishment in the different localities of the offices of *Sindaco* (mayor), of the *Presidente della Deputazione Provinciale* (President of the Provincial Council), assisted respectively by the *Giunta Municipale* (City Council) and the *Deputazione Provinciale* (Provincial Council), and of the election of members (except *ex-officio* members) to the *Giunta Provinciale Admininstrativa* (Provincial Administrative Committee).[3]

In this way a beginning was made to carry out the pro-

---

[1] *R.D.L.*, 11 February 1944, no. 32.

[2] *R.D.L.*, 4 April 1944, no. 111.

[3] The pre-Fascist system of local government in Italy was so totally unlike that of Great Britain that the translation of these titles can only be approximate. (*Translator*.)

gramme laid down by the First Council of Ministers; even in
matters where it was not possible to issue laws, the drafts which
were drawn up were of outstanding value to the successive
Cabinets, and formed a basis of subsequent legislation.

The internal consolidation of the State had important repercussions in the international sphere, and the consciousness of
duty done repaid the members of the Government for the
labours they undertook in the service of their country, while
convincing everyone that the Italian people were determined
to restore liberty and justice.

∾·   ∾·   ∾·

At the same time events of historic importance were about
to take place.

As soon as the passive resistance of the coalition parties
ceased and they were prepared to make their loyal contribution to the reconstruction of their country, the first Ministry
of Democratic Concentration came into existence. The new
Cabinet at once began to put its programme into effect.

It carried on the work of the former Ministry, adopted the
law dealing with sanctions against the crimes and the illegal
gains of the Fascists.[1] This law in addition to the previous
law for the purging of the personnel of the public services
(which the Coalition Ministry did not adopt although it was
ready) and other laws for the confiscation by the State of
illegal profits, constituted the basis of the law enacted by the
Bonomi Government on sanctions against Fascism.[2]

To emphasize the democratic character of the Cabinet, the
title of the 'Head of the Government' was changed during this
period to 'President of the Council of Ministers', in conformity
with the Italian liberal tradition.[3]

With the institution of a special Section of control of the
Corte dei Conti,[4] legal sanction was obtained for the work of

[1] *R.D.L.*, 26 May 1944, no. 134.
[2] *R.D.L.*, 26 May 1944, no. 134.
[3] *Decreto legislativo Luogotenenz*, 27 July 1944, no. 159.
[4] The body charged with the supervision of the Budget and the finances.
(*Translator.*)

the Government, for the budget,[1] and for the preparations for the calling of a Consultative Assembly to fill the gap left by the lack of a Parliament. The new political developments, however, did not allow these measures to be completed.

The Minister of Agriculture in agreement with the Allied Control Commission and with the approval of the Council of Ministers, created and controlled the working of the 'People's Granaries'. The sufferings of the working classes and of categories with fixed incomes caused by the blocking of wages and salaries, which was so rigidly enforced by the Allies, made it necessary to ensure a minimum ration, without obliging the Allies to import food.

Finally, I must mention because of its political importance, the law which forbade the inclusion in the *Reali Carabinieri* of undesirable elements from the road and port sections of the dissolved Fascist Militia.

It is not possible to give a comprehensive picture of the work of the Government during this tragic period of our national history, without an account of the rest of the legislative activity, which I have not already mentioned. I shall therefore summarize it in honour of those who laboured at it with such devotion.

The laws relating to the organization and working of the government departments, of the public bodies, and of legal institutions, were a prelude to the great reform made necessary by the change of policy; other laws had as their object the removal of difficulties to the development of the administrative machinery.

The following must also be mentioned:

Laws for the suppression of the Ministries of War Production,[2] of Exchange and Currency,[3] and of Popular Culture.

Laws for the temporary transfer during the state of war of

[1] *R.D.L.*, 29 May 1944, no. 141.
[2] *R.D.*, 27 January 1944, no. 24.
[3] *R.D.*, 2 June 1944, no. 150.

the Mercantile Marine from the Ministry of Communications to that of the Marine.[1]

Laws for the provisional transfer to the ministers or undersecretaries of the powers and functions belonging to collegiate bodies or individuals not able to exercise them.

Agreements necessary for the administration of public bodies[2] removing even formal reminders of the hateful past, such as the change of the name of the 'Commune of Mussolini' to that of Arborea.[3]

As I have explained, an effort at administrative decentralization was made by the appointment of High Commissioners for Sardinia[4] and for Sicily,[5] special consultative committees being set up to assist them, and also by the delegation of the maintenance of order and the co-ordination of local government.

Two other problems relating to social welfare were awaiting a solution: that of prisoners of war and that of the ever-growing numbers of refugees. A High Commissioner and a staff were appointed to deal with individual and collective questions relating to the status, treatment, employment, repatriation, and the moral and material condition of Italian prisoners and internees.[6]

A special section of the Ministry of Internal Affairs was set up to deal with refugees; but this soon proved inadequate and a new department was created with special powers and its own staff under a High Commissioner.[7]

---

[1] *R.D.L.*, 1 November 1943, no. 4B.

[2] *R.D.*, 2 February 1944, no. 62, relating to the control of naval hospitals; *R.D.*, 17 February 1944, no. 64, for the restoration of the Commune of Sarconi; *R.D.L.*, 13 April 1944, no. 118, for the modification of the boundaries of the Provinces of Matera and Potenza; *R.D.L.*, 27 January 1944, no. 23, for the Provincial Economic Councils; *R.D.L.*, 14 April 1944, no. 125, on the Communal Public Assistance Bodies; *R.D.*, 15 March 1944, no. 120, on Social Insurance; *R.D.L.*, 27 January 1944, no. 22, and 2 February 1944, no. 65, relating to the Bank of Naples.

[3] *R.D.*, 17 February 1944, no. 68.

[4] *R.D.L.*, 24 January 1944, no. 21, incorporated in *R.D.L.*, 16 March 1944, no. 90.   [5] *R.D.L.*, 18 March 1944, no. 91.

[6] *R.D.L.*, 6 April 1944, no. 107.

[7] *R.D.L.*, 29 May 1944, no. 137.

An increase in the salaries of the staffs of government offices and public bodies of about 70 per cent., with bonuses for length of service, was granted, within the limits imposed by the Allies.[1] The pay of the Pioneer Corps and also of the combatant units was raised.

In order to secure the services of all civil servants in the liberated territory those in the armed forces were released, and those who had abandoned their posts were ordered to report to the nearest prefects under threat of dismissal.[2] Owing to the lack of personnel and the increasing needs of the Government, retired employees were recalled[3] and others transferred from one department to another.[4]

It was necessary to modify the regulations for sequestrating, mortgaging, and blocking of stipends, salaries, and pensions paid by the State;[5] to suspend, for lack of senior officials, the functions of the Administrative Councils, of the Disciplinary Commissions, and the various Commissions dealing with staff matters in each Ministry;[6] to set up Provincial Commissions and give them temporary powers to deal with civil and military pensions, pending the re-establishment of the *Corte dei Conti* after the return of the Government to Rome.

Orders similar to those governing the salaries, &c., of government officials were enacted for the clergy[7] and for those employees whose wages were controlled by collective contracts.[8]

The economic legislation, within the draconian limits imposed by the situation, worked well.

[1] *R.D.L.*, 6 December 1943, no. 18B, for the salaries; *R.D.L.*, 9 May 1944, no. 131, for bonuses; *R.D.L.*, 13 March 1944, no. 85, for pensions; *R.D.L.*, 13 January 1944, no. 12, for increases of pay for the Air Force; *R.D.L.*, 23 March 1944, no. 3, for increases in Army pay.

[2] *R.D.L.*, 3 January 1944, no. 3, incorporated in *R.D.L.*, 8 June 1944, no. 148.

[3] Authorized by *R.D.L.*, 31 January 1944, no. 34.

[4] Authorized by *R.D.L.*, 31 January 1944, no. 55.

[5] *R.D.*, 20 January 1944, no. 43.

[6] *R.D.*, 12 April 1944, no. 109.

[7] *R.D.L.*, 24 January 1944, no. 19.

[8] *R.D.L.*, 7 December 1943, no. 23B.

The State, in order to create the necessary confidence in the work of reconstruction, provided proper guarantees for advances to industrial firms engaged in such work, granted tax exemptions, and even dealt with such matters as mortgages, sequestration, and alimony.[1] Other laws dealt with the payment of interest on Treasury Loans, with shares and other financial business transactions which could not be executed owing to a state of war and in which postponements were granted.[2]

Laws were passed putting an end to the contributions imposed on the professional classes for the World Exhibition in Rome and for the support of the Fascist Party.[3]

The prices of monopoly goods and the taxes on the importation of prepared tobacco were increased, a general import tax modifying the agreement for 1943 was passed, and the ban on liquors and alcohol was lifted in return for a contribution from the State.

Laws were enacted for the administration of justice. These arranged for the setting up of temporary courts at the seat of government, consisting of two sections of the Supreme Court of Cassation[4] and, in Lucera, of a section of the Court of Appeal,[5] and also for a recall of retired judges.[6] There were also important statutes such as that which confirmed the instructions already issued, sanctioning the suspension of trials in progress and the suspension of the Statute of Limitations. Another facilitated the civil and religious celebrations of marriages when it was impossible to observe the usual laws owing to the state of war.

In addition, greater guarantees of individual liberty were

---

[1] *R.D.L.*, 13 December 1943, no. 26B, incorporated in *R.D.L.*, 29 May 1944.

[2] *R.D.L.*, 6 December 1943, no. 19B, was extended to the territories restored to the Italian Government 6 April 1944, no. 115; *R.D.*, 6 December 1943, no. 20B.   [3] *R.D.L.*, 15 November 1943, no. 9B.

[4] *R.D.L.*, 8 April 1944, no. 100.

[5] *R.D.L.*, 20 January 1944, no. 27.

[6] *R.D.L.*, 20 January 1944, no. 28 (see also *R.D.L.*, 20 January 1944, no. 27).

provided by the reform of the laws dealing with prisoners awaiting trial in the civil courts, with those accused of being a danger to order or public security, and with the right of search of persons or of private premises.[1] As the Court of Appeal was unable to carry on its duties owing to the state of war, those whose cases were awaiting hearing were released provisionally.[2] Laws were adopted with regard to goods seized by order of the courts, and goods in short supply.[3]

To celebrate the return of the southern provinces and Sicily to Italian administration, an amnesty was granted for offences against civil and military codes, and for offences against the food laws.[4]

The interests of the legal profession were not overlooked, as is shown by the laws establishing special examinations for procurators, abrogating the age limit for notaries, and protecting lawyers who carried on their profession in the occupied territories.

Numerous laws dealt with army administration.[5] Among them one reorganizing the Carabinieri Reali[6] must be mentioned for its political and disciplinary importance; another awarded the good conduct medal, instituted for war volunteers, to civilian and military personnel who reached liberated territory after 8 September 1943 and reported for service.[7]

---

[1] *R.D.L.*, 20 January 1944, no. 45.

[2] *R.D.L.*, 20 January 1944, no. 42.

[3] *R.D.L.*, 20 January 1944, no. 44.

[4] *R.D.*, 5 April 1944, no. 96. See also *R.D.L.*, 8 April 1944, no. 99, modifying articles 593, and 595 of the C.P.P. allowing an act of clemency in all cases.

[5] *R.D.L.*, 18 November 1943, no. 10B, to set up an 'Inspectorate General of the Army'; *R.D.L.*, 3 January 1944, no. 7, alterations in the Commission dealing with promotion of officers in the Army during the war; *R.D.L.*, 3 January 1944, no. 8, constitution of the General Staff of the Army; *R.D.L.*, 17 February 1944, no. 73, regulations for the Commission controlling the promotion of officers in the Air Force during the war; *R.D.L.*, 2 March 1944, no. 79, alterations in the regulations dealing with the promotion of naval officers during the war.

[6] *R.D.L.*, 3 January 1944, no. 5 and *R.D.L.*, 3 January 1944, no. 6.

[7] *R.D.L.*, 27 January 1944, no. 54.

An especially important law in the field of public education was that which prohibited the use in the universities of books teaching Fascist ideology;[1] another re-established the equal rights for women to teach certain subjects and to hold certain positions in the schools. Steps were taken to meet the lack of teachers, and arrangements were made for students, so that they should not suffer from the unavoidable interruption of their studies.[2]

There was naturally little need for new legislation in connexion with public works and communications, but the Government could be proud of what it achieved in reconstruction and the re-establishment of public services. Every effort was made to keep motor vehicles of all kinds in good working order,[3] to organize the distribution of petrol, and to limit consumption by controlling the number of vehicles in use.[4]

Perhaps the clearest picture of the work of the various departments between September 1943 and June 1944, may be obtained by a list of the measures adopted and the instructions issued: more than 160 *provvedimenti legislativi*, 17 *bandi*, 39 *decreti reali*, 50 *decreti presidenziali*, 49 *decreti ministrali normativi*, besides departmental instructions and circular letters.[5] This list does not include laws which were prepared during this period and were put into execution by subsequent Cabinets.

[1] *R.D.*, 27 January 1944, no. 58.

[2] *R.D.L.*, 27 January 1944, no. 57, concerning the transfer of professors; *R.D.L.*, 16 March 1944, no. 114, authorizing the retention of professors who had reached the retiring age of 75; *R.D.L.*, 27 January 1944, no. 47, regulations for the matriculation and transfer of students from one university or college to another; *R.D.L.*, 27 January 1944, no. 48, and *R.D.*, 27 January 1944, no. 60, establishing respectively, special examinations and teaching courses for the academic year 1943–4 at the University of Bari; *R.D.*, 9 March 1944, no. 149, for the establishment of a teachers' training college at Salerno; *R.D.*, 27 January 1944, no. 49, exemptions from certain school fees to be extended for the year 1944.

[3] *R.D.L.*, 10 March, no. 83, and *R.D.L.*, 5 April 1944, no. 105.

[4] *R.D.L.*, 6 April, no. 106, and *R.D.L.*, 5 May 1944, no. 133. The *R.D.L.* of 9 May 1944, no. 143, authorized the Chief of the Civilian Engineering Staff to carry out urgent work up to the cost of 200,000 lire.

[5] This list covers laws, orders, ministerial decrees of various kinds for which there are no equivalent legal terms in English. (*Translator.*)

With exiguous resources and an almost total lack of trained personnel, the Government was called upon to organize an efficient central administration. This was essential if the civilian population was to be provided with the means to lead a normal life, in so far as was compatible with a state of war and the terrible destruction which it brought in its train. In the political sphere Fascism had to be eliminated and the democratic form of government re-established.

The Cabinet worked untiringly to attain these ends, and the results show that its labours were not in vain. What was left undone was not for lack of goodwill but for lack of time, and others have built on the foundations which were laid.

Everyone who bore his share of the burden may be proud of the fact that he made his contribution to the future well-being of his country.

INDEX

PRINTED IN
GREAT BRITAIN
AT THE
UNIVERSITY PRESS
OXFORD
BY
CHARLES BATEY
PRINTER
TO THE
UNIVERSITY